THE I

HEALTHY GUINEA

PIG GUIDEBOOK

The Ultimate Step-By-Step Guide for a No Mess, Zero Stress Guinea Pig Owning Experience

Lucy Meadway

Published by WriterMotive
www.writermotive.com

Praise for The Happy, Healthy Guinea Pig Guidebook

"Look no further for the definitive guide to guinea pig ownership. As a vet and guinea pig owner, I find many uninitiated guinea pig owners struggle to understand their complex needs, which can be hard to explain within the limitations of a 10 minute consultation. This is THE perfect, well-researched resource to direct them to. Even the most seasoned guinea pig lover will find some valuable nuggets of information here."

Ben Simpson-Vernon aka Ben the Vet

"Lucy shares her wealth of experience in this informative, down-to-earth look at the joys and pitfalls of guinea pig ownership, which both new and existing piggy parents will find invaluable, as they strive to provide the best care for happy and healthy guinea pigs."

Angela Harding — C&C Guinea Pig Cages
www.candcguineapigcages.co.uk

"Lucy has done an amazing job at putting together a comprehensive book that covers every aspect of guinea pig care with advice that is spot on and presented in an amusing, easy-to-read fashion. Jim and I have rescued and re-homed thousands of guinea pigs over two decades through our charity Bobtails Rabbit and Guinea Pig Rescue, and we are delighted that Lucy has included information that seems to be missed in many guinea pig care guides that we so often have to inform or correct prospective adopters about who have been misinformed.

We thoroughly enjoyed reading it and advise anyone thinking of having piggies join their family to read this book first. This book tells it like it is, with the many ups, but also the downs of guinea pig ownership. It is a brilliant read for new and existing owners. Everyone can learn from Lucy's book!"

Delia and Jim Cordell, founders of Bobtails Rabbit and Guinea Pig Rescue, Surrey
www.bobtailsrescue.org.uk

"There is a wealth of useful information in this book for the first-time guinea pig owner. There are many guinea pig care books available, but many of them have not been updated since they were written many years ago. Out-of-date information can be confusing and may even be detrimental to the health and happiness of your precious guinea pigs. Over the past 20 years of keeping guinea pigs, and running Gorgeous Guineas since 2003, I have seen many changes and improvements in things such as veterinary care, new types of bedding, and much more interest in different types of hay and herbs that are so important for their health. It is so important to do your research before getting any pet, and this book covers all the most important considerations before you get your first guinea pigs.

This book would make a good starting point for anyone considering getting guinea pigs as pets. Lucy provides different options for things like food and bedding; no two homes are the same, and no one solution works for every set up."

Chrissie Slade, owner of Gorgeous Guineas
www.gorgeousguineas.com

"This is a fantastic, and modern guinea pig guide from Lucy! I run a pet hotel service for rabbits, guinea pigs and hamsters and I never tire of meeting all our lovely animal guests and getting to know their different characters and preferences whilst they are here on holiday at the pet hotel!

Many adults today had rabbits and guinea pigs themselves as children, and often carry on with those out-of-date care methods that were learnt many years ago when they decide to get guinea pigs for their own children. But in fact, today, things have changed so much, now we have learnt so much more about these amazing little animals!

One of the things that saddens me in my job is meeting so many gorgeous guinea pigs but hearing from the families that the novelty and interest can quickly wear off, but with Lucy's book and enthusiasm you will get plenty of ideas and inspiration for housing and their daily care so your guinea pigs will be enjoying their lives in a spacious and fun set up, meaning they will be happy piggies that the whole family can appreciate, enjoy and include as very much part of the family."

Kerry Salton, owner of Kerry's Pets
www.kerryspets.co.uk

"This book is a comprehensive care guide that will help so many people give their guinea pigs the best life possible. While reading this book, I found myself nodding in agreement frequently. As a long-standing volunteer at The Los Angeles Guinea Pig Rescue, I have seen and heard almost everything you could imagine from strange and unique rescues, rare and common illnesses to success and horror stories which I share plenty on my YouTube channel 'Scotty's Animals' which is dedicated to helping animals in need and those who care for them; that is why I'm so excited about this book and grateful to Lucy for writing it. Just like human parenting, we all have different styles and dispositions, which this book allows for, while providing a solid foundation of care and explanations that are clear. This book is a great resource for new and longtime guinea pig parents. As Lucy explains, so much has changed over the years about how we care for guinea pigs and what is understood and agreed upon, and it's constantly changing. The best piggy parents keep an open heart and mind. This book explains concepts about guinea pig care in ways that will empower us to keep learning for a lifetime. This is a must have guinea pig care guide!"

Scott Hale, Scotty's Animals on YouTube, Guinea Pig Rescue Volunteer

"*The Healthy, Happy Guinea Pig* is the ultimate guide to guinea pig care. Taking you through setting up your piggies' home, to choosing the best combination of pigs for you, Lucy's book ensures you are prepared for your new little critters. A must-read if you are considering owning guinea pigs."

Abbie Rutherford
www.abbie-editorial.com

Contents

Introduction

"Why can't the world be simpler, like it is for guinea pigs? They only have a few rules: Crying will get you attention. If it fits in your mouth, it's food. Scream if you don't get your share."

Cynthia Lord

I remember the day I took home my first guinea pigs Onyx and Luna, who are still with me today. It was a bit of a rush; I'd been thinking about getting guinea pigs for a while and had done a lot of research, but when I saw them that day in the adoption section in the pet store and saw that they'd been waiting for a home for months; I couldn't say no! I quickly got together the basics I needed for them and one of the largest cages there, which I knew, sadly, still wasn't big enough. The thought that they might end up somewhere else in the cage the store deemed suitable for their entire lives was enough for me to take them home immediately.

Once home, I let them settle in by leaving them alone whilst I prepped for the correct sized cage, which I could not buy in any local store. I don't think I even saw them come out from hiding for a few days, and I worried they were too scared to eat. I spent forever trawling through the internet to find the right cage, and within a week they were sorted. But this rushing around meant that although they had everything they needed after the first week, I was spending a lot more time cleaning them out than I thought: the set-up was awkward and I had no idea how much they pooed (they miss that one out a lot when they tell you about guinea pigs, but I won't, don't worry!).

Well, I'm glad to say, they've turned into the most confident little critters who love cuddles, exploring in their big cage, and cleaning them out is now a breeze; but it has taken me a good few years to really get into such a good routine that caring for them is a breeze whilst I work full time, run Little Critter Care and have even introduced a 3 rd guinea pig to the herd and the rest of the gang, the hamsters.

So, I'm here to share everything I've learnt – the good, the bad and the ugly – to make your guinea pig owning experience a breeze from the very start.

Life with guinea pigs is awesome; they're quite happy to be lap pets, but will also run around, explore and interact with one another, they don't mind being left for the day while you're at work but will 'wheek' with excitement at the prospect of fresh food from their human when you come in through the door. For someone like me, who loves animals but has a schedule far too busy for a dog of my own, guinea pigs have been the perfect fit and I've been able to provide 5 gorgeous guineas in need of a home with all the love and care they need. However, man can they be hard work and the amount a small creature can poo still amazes me.

Guinea pigs come across as these simple creatures with basic needs, however, new owners can soon realise they're not quite as easy as described in the pet store…

Keeping them clean and tidy, not realising the space they need, and struggling to tame these small and timid little critters is something that new owners can struggle with.

And if you get guinea pig ownership wrong by keeping them in too small a space, not providing them the right nutrition or company of their own kind, not taming or grooming them, you'll end up with sad, smelly guinea pigs who constantly hide from you and could cost you an awful lot in vet bills.

Sadly, many guinea pigs end up in rescues; thousands are currently in rescues across the UK and some of the most common reasons for this are that the children have become bored of them, someone in the house is allergic to them, or the owners simply don't have time for them. More often than not, this could be prevented, and in this book you'll find everything you need to know to keep happy, healthy guinea pigs with no mess and less stress as an owner.

* * *

But firstly, are you ready for guinea pigs? Are they the right pets for you?

There was certainly a time years ago, when I was looking into getting guinea pigs, I'd been watching a popular YouTuber who has guinea pigs and they looked so easy to care for; didn't seem to need much time or space and were happy being picked up and stroked. After doing some research I found that they needed lots more space, they live far longer than the average rodents and they would take up quite a bit of time. I decided they just weren't right for me yet. I was living in a rented flat that didn't have enough space, and I wasn't quite sure where I'd be in a year or so's time, though I had just started my job as a secondary school teacher. Guinea pigs typically live between 4 and 7 years, so I knew that would pretty much cancel any plans for long holidays or travels. I had a hamster and although they are simpler to care for and require less space (though still far more than you would think), they aren't awake during the day like guinea pigs are. For me, guinea pigs provide affection that hamsters don't. That

11

being said, many owners are disappointed when they find that their guinea pigs run away from them, squeal when they're picked up and are difficult to handle.

You might see images on social media of guinea pigs loving cuddles, chin scratches and confidently running to their owners for vegetables, however, this isn't the reality for all guinea pigs and can take days, months or years to achieve.

One of my favourite things about guinea pigs is their individual personalities; no one guinea pig is the same and you will quickly learn their little quirks. It's what, in my opinion, makes guinea pigs one of the most special little critters out there. Be aware that this also means that some guinea pigs will always be shy, some will be bossy and always first to the food, some will screech when they're picked up but lie flat as a pancake in relaxation as you stroke them on your lap.

* * *

There are 4 fundamental things you need to have if you're thinking about having guinea pigs:

Time, patience, space and money.

Time is for cleaning them out, buying their food and bedding, taking them into a play pen for some enrichment and not to mention needing to make sure you're at home at least part of each day for them.

Patience is for taming them and simply caring for them over the months where you may not get much back from them. They will run and hide and you might think they even dislike you for a while; are you prepared for this?

Space: guinea pigs need a lot more space than is shown in your average pet store. There is a whole chapter in this book about all you need to know on this.

Money is for lots of food (they eat a lot of hay and need fresh vegetables every day), bedding (did I mention how much they poo?) and vet bills. Now you might be thinking a couple of hundred will do the job, but wait until you read about my story about how much I spent on Wiggy last year later in the book.

If you read this book and decide that guinea pigs aren't for you, then I salute you. Guinea pigs aren't for everyone and sometimes they're just not for right now.

But first, who am I to tell you what to do with your new pig?

Well, I'm Lucy Meadway, better known as Little Critter Lucy! Besides my own critters, I help lots of owners with their own pets, whether that's helping to trim the claws of skittish rabbits and guinea pigs, providing expert care when owners are away, or giving help and advice on easiest and best care for their pets. I even appeared on BBC Radio Kent recently to discuss some of the misconceptions of rabbit ownership after I raised money for a local rabbit and guinea pig rescue. Guinea pigs, rabbits and hamsters are some of the most common, yet misunderstood pets in the UK and I've made it my mission to make sure they're cared for as well as our beloved cats and dogs.

* * *

Are you ready to learn how to have happy, healthy guinea pigs?

In this book, you'll find everything you need to know about keeping guinea pigs from a practical perspective. What you won't find is information about the history of guinea pigs, all about the different breeds or how to breed guinea pigs.

You also won't find me telling you only one way of doing things; people have different lives, living situations and budgets and there are many different ways of meeting the same needs. This book will show you a variety of ways of coming to a solution and is all about making guinea pig ownership less stressful for you without compromising your guinea pigs' happiness. I don't want owners to struggle with their guinea pigs only to surrender them to a rescue when there are plenty of simple fixes to common guinea pig problems. Some things in this book you might not agree with, or find challenging to what you've previously been told, but rest assured everything in this book has guinea pigs' best interests at heart and will make owning them easier.

And if you're reading this book in 2030 – please put the thing down immediately! Pet care is constantly evolving, and where you may read a book from the 90s that says it's OK to keep them in a tiny hutch outside, that doesn't mean that's the current advice.

There is so much outdated advice out there still being given, whether it is from large chain pet shops, or even experienced breeders. Things have come a long way over the years, and I genuinely hope that things will keep moving forward.

There are, however, things in this book that may never change, whether it is diet or taming.

Rest assured, all of the advice in this book has come from years of research and experience, and keeping up to date with the latest and best advice.

And everything I recommend is easy to do.

This book will provide you with everything you need to know before and during your guinea pig owning experience that has the well-being of guinea pigs at its core. It will take you on a journey, from deciding on whether they're the right pets for you, to how to care for them throughout their lives.

So, lets dive into Chapter 1 where you'll discover whether guinea pigs are the right pets for you...

CHAPTER 1
Are Guinea Pigs the Right Pets for Me?

Before we kick off with everything you need to know about caring for guinea pigs, I'm going to go through some common questions people ask, or should have asked, before getting guinea pigs.

In this chapter I'll be going through some of the common misconceptions of guinea pig ownership and help you decide whether they're the right pets for you.

Whilst you'll find a lot more information in this book about diet, what space they need and how to keep them healthy, let's go through some honest answers about caring for guinea pigs.

Now remember, I love guinea pigs and wouldn't dream of a life without them, but they're not for everyone and here's why…

Are they good pets for children?

When I was about 4, I'd been begging my parents for a rabbit. Finally, they gave in and adopted Pepper. I loved Pepper to bits and still remember her well, but was I responsible at looking after her? No. And I really have been animal obsessed my whole life, from feeding the ducks before I can even remember to trying to save a bee in the back garden. However, I wasn't (even into my teenage years) able to understand how important it was to clean out, feed and check on her every single day, especially when I was wanting to hang out with my friends on weekends and avoiding chores at all costs. Sadly, as much as I loved her, Pepper became a chore. Fortunately, my mum wanted her too and spent a lot more time caring for her than I did, and she still keeps rabbits 25 years later!

So, do you want the honest answer…? *No* pets are good pets for children. It is so important that any pets are wanted by at least one adult in the household, because children won't be able to foot a vet bill that might be into the hundreds of pounds, they might simply get bored, or maybe they will even go off to university whilst their pets are still alive.

But that's not to say that guinea pigs specifically are a bad choice for a family that have children, in fact they can be the perfect pets.

Safety is an important factor when deciding on which pet to get when you have children. Biting can be one of the main concerns when choosing a pet.

So… do guinea pigs bite?

Well yes, they can, but they are one of the least likely pets to bite. I've worked with all sorts of animals from rabbits and cats to hamsters and foxes. And I can honestly say that of all the animals I've worked with, guinea pigs on the whole are the gentlest. It would take a lot for a guinea pig to bite, and it would only be out of pure fear and defence, which is actually like most animals, and their first instinct is to run away. With the guidance from this book you should never find yourself in a position where your guinea pig needs to be this frightened.

However, because of this possibility, that's why it's so important to teach children how to handle them correctly and not to do anything that might make your guinea pig feel unsafe.

There are plenty of fun things to do with guinea pigs and children, whether it's spending time making guinea pig houses from cardboard boxes, or settling down to cuddle with them on the sofa.

Do they like to be stroked?

Guinea pigs often like to be stroked, though not always, and especially not when you first bring them home, so patience is something that's really needed here. Be prepared for it to take months to tame them, as sometimes children and parents get disheartened when they find their new adorable pets always want to run away and hide, but with the right environment (as I will explain in Chapter 7), they will build up confidence and really come out of their shells.

A child under the age of 10 should not pick up a guinea pig, but they would quite comfortably be able to sit down to stroke a guinea pig on their lap with supervision.

The real question is, are they right for you and will they fit in with your family life? You'll have to read the rest of the chapter to find out…

How much time do guinea pigs require?

Now, I get to visit and care for lots of animals. Some days I might see 4 guinea pigs, 2 rabbits, 3 dogs, 2 cats and 5 chickens. I have a pretty good idea of the time involved with each and of course over the years I've become very efficient with my routines, but I would certainly say guinea pigs are up there with the most time consuming. When it comes to cleaning out, only the chickens could rival them. As for the hay, didn't I literally just top that up?

That being said, with the right advice your daily routine could easily consist of a 5-minute top up of food, change of water and check-up in the morning, and a 5–10-minute vegetable dinner and a quick spot clean. Then there's the weekly (or possibly even bi-weekly) big clean! This can be anywhere from 20 minutes to an hour depending on how efficient your routine is. I know plenty of people that need to do full cleans every few days even.

Of course, there's the extra time you'll want to spend with them whether that's on your lap or in a play pen.

The time you spend buying their supplies and end up spending an extra hour in the pet store looking at all the cool things you can buy for them.

And don't forget your personal time when you get invited out for an impromptu weekend getaway; 'I can't, sorry, my guinea pigs will need their veggies this evening and I can't find anyone to look after them last minute.'

If you already own pets, you'll have some sense of this, but losing some freedom with pet ownership is always worth being aware of. I find guinea pigs to be easier than dogs in this sense as they don't mind being left during the day.

How much do they cost?

Guinea pigs themselves are cheap to buy or adopt and are typically sold for about £20. Unlike dogs, who can sell for thousands, these seem incredibly cheap in comparison.

However, it's important to factor in the ongoing costs of keeping them.

Besides the initial outlay for a cage and basic supplies, you'll have the monthly reoccurring costs for food (including fresh vegetables), bedding (you'll use so much more than you would litter for a cat – I throw away a sack full a week easily), and not to mention, vet bills.

Now you might not think vet bills would get big with small animals, but since they're classed as exotics, you'll often find yourself paying more for an exotic vet due to their extra training. If you want to know more about the cost of your guinea pig's health and how much one of my guinea pigs set me back, there's plenty in Chapter 9.

Not only do you need money now, but you need this on a regular basis for potentially 7 or more years depending on how long you have your guinea pigs around for. Of course, nobody can guarantee income like this, but can you be fairly confident you can afford them in the long run?

Am I going to be allergic to guinea pigs?

This is one of the most common reasons guinea pigs end up in rescues, and one that could be easily avoided.

Don't forget that although you might not be allergic, someone in your household might be.

Before deciding on getting guinea pigs, I would highly recommend visiting your local rescue with your household and getting covered in fur.

Also, a crucial part of a guinea pig's diet is hay, so please consider this if you suffer with hay fever.

That's not to say there aren't guinea pig owners out there without allergies, but you definitely need to have a die-hard love for piggies to deal with the rashes, and be prepared to find solutions to the constant sneezing.

Can guinea pigs live with other pets?

Before you decide to get guinea pigs, one of the things you should consider is whether you have any other pets in the house; in particular, pets that are considered predators to guinea pigs.

You may not think loving, friendly dog Fido, or fluffy Felix the cat would hurt more than a fly, but unfortunately, I have heard too many horror stories not to include this warning in the book.

Dogs, cats, ferrets, rats and, believe it or not, rabbits have been known to harm, and even kill guinea pigs. Equally, I visit lots of different families with a multitude of pets and I have also witnessed dogs being very calm around their guinea pigs, though I don't know anyone who ever leaves them together unsupervised.

Can't rabbits and guinea pigs live together? I've seen them living happily together in farms...

This is a common misconception amongst many, since it didn't used to be too unusual to house them together. However, they not only both have different dietary requirements, but rabbits are bigger and can bully and seriously injure guinea pigs. There are also certain bacteria rabbits carry that cause no harm to the rabbit but can be passed on to guinea pigs and cause serious illness. For this reason, it is strongly advised to keep rabbits and guinea pigs separate.

Will guinea pigs benefit from interaction with other pets?

The bottom line is no; different species really offer no value to guinea pigs. Guinea pigs gain so much from interaction with their own kind that if you are concerned that your guinea pig might be lonely, then the best thing to do is seek out another guinea pig for company (see more of this in Chapter 10). For this reason, I see no need to risk introduction with another species.

This doesn't, however, mean you can't happily have a multi pet household.

Two ways to keep your guinea pigs safe from other pets within your household:

- Make sure their cage is secure and has a lid; cats are great at opening cages, so I'd even recommend a padlock or reusable cable ties just to be on the safe side.
- Keep them in a separate part of the house to other pets altogether; consider always keeping their door shut or locked, or have a child gate at the door to keep small dogs out.

Please be aware that accidents can happen. Despite me building a lid to my hamster's tank to make sure she can't escape, there was a time when my partner left the lid off one day, and another time she bit herself out and had a nice run around the house and found the nuts in the kitchen cupboard. If you forget to shut the door one day, will your dog – who you know loves to chase after rabbits in the woods – be straight in there? Will the rest of your household take the separation of pets seriously enough?

These are just some things to consider in the huge variety of situations there might be.

Chapter summary

Guinea pigs can make excellent pets, but they're not right for everyone and they're certainly not the ultimate 'starter pet'. They're so much more than that in good, and some bad, ways.

Before taking home a pair or more of guinea pigs, remember to go through some of the common reasons that guinea pigs are handed to rescue centres across the globe, and ask yourself the following questions:

- 'Am I prepared to commit to looking after my guinea pigs or are they simply for the children?'
- 'Can I be patient and be fine with guinea pigs that might not like to be stroked?'
- 'Do I have the time, daily, to care for them?'
- 'Can I afford regular food, bedding and sometimes unexpected vet bills?'
- 'Could I be allergic to guinea pigs?'
- 'Can I keep them safe from other pets in my home?'

Once you've passed each of those, you're more than ready to get stuck into the rest of the book, where you'll find out everything you need to know about keeping piggies in this easy-peasy guide.

WARNING: Guinea pigs can be addictive. Guinea pig ownership will also require the willpower to not bring home any more than you have the space, money and time for.

CHAPTER 2
How to Pick the Right Guinea Pigs

So, you've pretty much decided you want guinea pigs, but just don't know where to start. Boys, girls, older, younger, different breeds, etc. There are so many things to consider, particularly what will fit in best with your lives. You might even be thinking to yourself 'Why does that even matter? Aren't they all the same?'

When people decide to bring a dog into their home, there are careful considerations to make about which dog will suit their lifestyle and which they can also provide a suitable home for. If you simply don't have time to spend 2+ hours a day exercising and want a dog to provide company who preferably needs minimal exercise, you're not going to bring home a young, high energy Border Collie!

In this chapter, I will be guiding you through the differences between breed, age and gender of guinea pigs, along with how many you might consider keeping and where to get them from in order to make sure you and your guinea pigs are a good fit.

Breeds

If you want a thorough guide on breeds, I'm afraid this isn't it. I'm not all that into breeds or are bothered by which colour they are or how spikey their hair is. Maybe you are, and that's fine. However, it is important to understand some basic needs that will differ with different breeds, as some can require more care than others.

A lot of the guinea pigs you see in pet stores have **short, smooth coats**, and come in a variety of colours. These require the lowest maintenance as their fur stays the same length and they generally stay clean. Names for these breeds are **American** and **Crested** guinea pigs. Often, guinea pigs sold in pet stores and in rescues are a mix of these breeds as they are ideal for beginners.

Abyssinian guinea pigs have slightly longer coats that have rosettes or 'cow licks' that make their hair flick in different directions. They are also low maintenance, but you may find they are less likely to enjoy being stroked because of the different directions of their hair growth. That being said, Sullivan was an aby and loved a head scratch!

Long-haired guinea pigs come in many varieties. Some might have hair that's straight and smooth, or wild and curly. Some of these breeds are known as Peruvian, Silkie, Texel and many more. These guinea pigs will require regular brushing, sometimes daily. Many people also trim the hair to stop it dragging along the floor as this will often become covered in urine. It is important to consider if you have the time and confidence to handle these high mainte-nance piggies.

Hairless guinea pigs, often known as a 'skinny pigs'; you either love them already or you're about to google one and be horrified by this strange-looking creature. Although no brushing is needed since they have almost no hair, their exposed, delicate skin will need some extra care by staying away from wood shavings and opting for fleece instead and the occasional massage of coconut oil. If you're planning on keeping your guinea pigs outside, a skinny pig is not for you. It is worth researching more thoroughly if you're considering getting a skinny.

Satin guinea pigs are known for their super shiny hair that is unmistakable in sunlight but can be difficult to see in a photo. This is one breed I would be very careful about considering, particularly when buying from a store or breeder. Without going into too much detail, osteodystrophy (OD) is a bone disease that is only found within guinea pigs that carry the satin gene. This is often known as 'satin syndrome'. The gene can be crossed with different breeds e.g., a satin silkie. That is not to say that any guinea pig with the satin gene will get OD. Satin breeding is banned in Finland and Sweden who have particularly high standards of guinea pig care. You may well find a satin carrier in need of a home from a rescue that will inform you of any health problems.

There are lots more breeds and cross breeds of guinea pigs. Many people will claim that certain breeds have more friendly personalities, but in my experience, they often break the stereotype on this so you're best off judging their personalities when you meet them.

If you see an unusual breed not mentioned here that takes your fancy, ask an expert to identify the breed and do some research to check whether they require any sort of extra care so that you're prepared.

Having higher maintenance guinea pigs can be great fun; I loved trimming Wiggy's hair (though he definitely didn't!), and knowing I had the time and confidence to do this was an important factor in my decision to adopt him. He hated being brushed so I cut his hair shorter so that he didn't have to face this ordeal as often.

Age

Snowball the guinea pig is in the *Guinness Book of World Records 1979* for being the oldest piggie to have lived at a whopping 14 years and 10 months old!

Your average guinea pig, however, lives for 5 to 7 years.

Age is definitely something to consider when choosing your new guinea pigs. Where do you see yourself in 5 years' time? Do you have teenage children keen to go to university in a couple of years who are desperate for guinea pigs? Maybe you have young children and have no plans to move until they've left home. Maybe you're a woman in your 30s, like me, who is quite happy to be a crazy guinea pig lady for the next 30 years or so.

Of course, nobody really knows what's ahead of them, but it's good to consider where things might be and what your plans are.

You will find all sorts of ages of guinea pigs in rescues. Sullivan had just turned 4 when I adopted him, and was sadly outlived even by my hamsters.

There can be pros and cons to adopting guinea pigs of different ages, besides the simple matter of time you have with them.

Young guinea pigs under 6 months:

Many people are tempted by young guinea pigs, and they are often the only option in a pet store. However, as adorable as they are when they're this young, they come with some challenges.

They are the most skittish and difficult to tame. Remember that image you had of chilling with them on your lap while you both watch TV? Forget it, at least for the first few months.

Beware of young boy pairs, there is a good possibility they will fall out during puberty, and you will need to be prepared for the potential fallout.

If you have a C&C cage, you will have to make sure the grids are small enough or put up a temporary barrier to make sure their heads do not get stuck. This is easy enough to do but can be a hassle if you're looking for a stress-free guinea pig owning experience.

On the plus side, the younger the guinea pig, the more likely you are to have them in your family longer. You will be able to experience the different stages of their lives and this is when they are most active and excitable.

Older guinea pigs:

Seven months is by no means old for a guinea pig, but you are more likely to find this age group or older at a rescue or store adoption section.

With many things in life, we often assume that because something is older and second-hand that it holds less value.

With rescue dogs, for example, it is often assumed that they might have a problem too deep-rooted to fix, and many owners buy puppies in the hope of starting from scratch, training early and hoping to avoid any potential problems.

But like a good winc, guinea pigs get better with age!

They are one of the gentlest pets you can have, and despite their initial timidness, they're real characters and aren't phased by much. They get used to their surroundings and in a safe environment quickly learn to trust their owners, particularly as they get older.

Of course, older age can come with its downsides too; they might be more likely to have health problems and you might have to prepare for them to not be around for as long as you might like. Equally, you could adopt a young guinea pig and still have sudden illness at a young age (and I'll tell you more about my Christmas Day at the emergency vet with Wiggy in Chapter 9), but it's worth taking into consideration, nonetheless.

Genders – girls or boys? What's the difference?

Although every guinea pig has an individual personality, there are some things you might want to consider when choosing the gender of your guinea pigs, especially if you are new to ownership.

There is no clear difference between the genders with regards to their temperaments, though many say that male guinea pigs, known as 'boars', are generally more relaxed, with females, known as 'sows', being more skittish. Boys will likely also be more dominant, and this can cause some difficult dynamics which I'll explain on page 18.

In my own experience, Onyx my female guinea pig has been the most wanting of human affection and loves nothing better than lying down with her legs kicked to one side having a head rub and chin stroke. So, take this all with a pinch of salt, use them as general guidelines and make sure you meet your potential guinea pigs first and judge their personalities for yourself.

The main difference worth noting is that a pair of boars requires a larger space than a pair of sows. But read on to this very important next section, where I explain about pairings and the problems that can arise. The gender of your guinea pigs certainly can play an important factor in your experience of owning guinea pigs.

How to tell them apart

I've heard many pet shop and breeder miss-sexing stories. Rescues are usually on the ball with this and are super careful so as not to have even more guinea pigs to look after and find homes for.

If you find yourself stuck in a situation where you might be wondering whether you have a same sex pair, then this diagram might be useful in helping you avoid having pregnant guinea pigs.

Male (boar)	Female (sow)
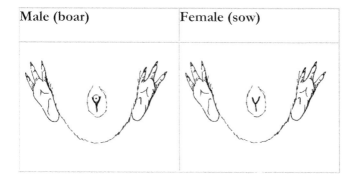	

A guinea pig's gender can be very difficult to tell from a diagram and comes with experience. If you're unsure and have reasons to believe you have guinea pigs of a different sex living together, separate them if you can and contact your vet or local rescue for help with this. Another way to tell if your guinea pig is male is to press carefully, but somewhat firmly, above where the penis is, and the penis will pop out. It looks quite silly but if you see this, it is a way of being certain. If not, it could be that you're not pressing in the right place, or that they're female.

Can I just get one guinea pig? Do they need friends?

In the wild, guinea pigs live in herds, and like many other groups of animals, have a hierarchy. Domestic guinea pigs establish this too, where one guinea pig will be the boss. If 2 guinea pigs want to be the boss, this can cause problems.

You will likely hear from pet shops that if they stay with their cage mate from a young age they will continue to get along, but that's not entirely true. Guinea pigs can be fussy about who they live with, and it's common for boys once they hit puberty to fight over dominance, resulting in separation. You are, however, less likely to get this with girls.

That's not to say you can't have boys who get along great, or girls that won't fall out.

Here is a list of pairings that do and don't work well together:

DO	DON'T
2 or more girls	3 or more boys
1 neutered boy with 1 or more girls	Unneutered boy with un-spayed girl
2 boys	2 or more unneutered boys with 1 or more girls

These are a general rule, and although you might hear of people who have groups of boys, that's not to say they're doing anything wrong, it's just not easy to find matches that way. But this book isn't 'How to make guinea pig ownership as challenging as possible'.

The pairings that almost always work out are girls, or a neutered boy with 1 or more girls (see Chapter 9 for advice on neutering).

Male pairings can be great, and males themselves are often said to be more friendly with humans. It can be a good choice, especially if you want to keep 2 guinea pigs only. But beware of puberty, which hits at 2–3 months old and can last for 8–10 months.

What's the best way to ensure I choose a pair of guinea pigs that are likely to stay friends?

Adopting an already bonded pair past puberty at the age of around 1 year old or older is a good start. Going through a reputable rescue is ideal if you are a new owner, as you will be able to skip the awkward teenage phase, help guinea pigs in need of a home, and receive advice and guidance from that rescue should there be any falling out at a later stage.

As you become more experienced, or can provide separate housing and take on more guinea pigs as potential matches for your separated guinea pigs, you might then be comfortable choosing a slightly gutsier sow pairing or 4-month-old boars.

It is always worth considering that the average pet shop won't help should there be a falling out with your guinea pigs, though an experienced breeder should, and rescues certainly will. Ask them what you can do if they don't get along. If the store, breeder or rescue is not willing to help find a solution, that's a red flag and best avoided so make sure you ask this question before you buy.

Wherever you decide to get your guinea pigs, consider the potential for what you might do should there be a falling out. More in Chapter 10.

Shop or adopt?

If you've learnt a little about me already, one thing you'll know is that I absolutely love guinea pigs; not simply for me to get satisfaction from them, but I love seeing them get the most from their lives. And as much as I love my own guinea pigs, I care deeply for the many guinea pigs around the world that I will never get to meet.

One of my main goals with this book is to make guinea pig ownership simple and enjoyable enough that more will be adopted, and less will be given up to rescues. Rescues are always bursting at the seams, so I hope this book can grant them even a small reprieve.

Whilst there are still hundreds, if not thousands, of guinea pigs in rescues across the UK alone, I will always only advocate for adopting guinea pigs from rescues.

The benefits of adopting from a rescue are also better not only for guinea pigs but for yourself too. Rescues will usually provide health checks from a vet before you pick them up; they will make sure they are the correct sex (they certainly don't want to be paying for more babies!); and will provide you with longer support should you need to give them up later down the line due to unforeseen circumstances.

One thing rescues will do that, often, pet shops and breeders won't, is to request a home check before you take your guinea pigs home. This is a simple process that can often be done virtually but means that the rescue is making sure their guinea pigs are going to be well cared for. But don't worry, this book is going to give you everything you need to do to wow your local rescue without the stress.

Chapter Summary

Choosing your first, or any additional guinea pigs is an important step and can make a difference in your guinea pig owning experience. I've sometimes impulsively taken in a pet that wasn't a great fit because I didn't think it through and I let the cuteness take over; I'd really recommend having some time beforehand to think logically about what is right for you.

My key tip from this chapter is to adopt from your local rescue. Not only will they find the right breed and age to suit you, but it will come with the help and support that you won't get if you buy from a pet shop.

Remember to always take home at least a pair of guinea pigs, but no more than 2 if you're getting only males. If you have the support of a rescue behind you then absolutely consider taking a pair of males home as they're more likely to have been paired up very well.

And don't be afraid to go for a slightly older pair; they will have an established relationship unlikely to break, and they will be less likely to be skittish.

The most important thing to remember is that they all have such individual personalities that they will quickly break these stereotypes. So, use this as a guide to get you started and have a think before you see that gorgeous guinea pig that must be yours.

CHAPTER 3
What Should I Feed My Guinea Pig?

Now I'm not exactly sure why guinea pigs are called guinea 'pigs', but one obvious reason would be that they are greedy pigs! They absolutely love to eat, which can be great, especially for working on taming (more of that later in the book) because you will be the bearer of everything they love.

Their diet consists of lots of hay (completely endless access 24/7), dried pellets full of what they need, and fresh vegetables. They also need constant access to fresh water. With so many different types of hay and pellets, and so much conflicting advice on vegetables it can be an absolute minefield! Then when you do eventually find the right stuff, they end up being picky eaters and you're back to square one researching the best food.

Here is a simple guide to choosing the best food for you and your guinea pigs.

Pellets:

There are so many different types around that it can be difficult to know which to buy. They also don't need a full bowl, only really a handful each per day of nutritious pellets – you want them to be mainly eating hay, and not be filling up on pellets. Here are some key points when choosing a brand of pellets for your guinea pigs:

1. Always opt for pellets/nuggets instead of muesli mix. With muesli mixes guinea pigs can be pickier

about what they eat and won't necessarily get the full benefit of the food.

2. Some of the budget pellets are full of cheap ingredients such as soy and wheat which have very little to no nutritional value to guinea pigs; they're just to bulk the food out. Some also contain a lot of alfalfa (also known as 'lucerne') which you want to try to avoid in adult guinea pigs since it can lead to too much calcium in some guinea pigs which can make them ill.

3. Give the ingredients list a quick check, the main ingredient is always the first, then followed by the second, and so on.

4. The first ingredient should be grass or hay (any type except for alfalfa).

5. The following ingredients are OK, but preferably further down the list: alfalfa (lucerne), soy, wheat and molasses (sugar).

Stick with these 5 points and you'll be able to find something at your local store, even if you've not got access to the best selection.

Don't be put off by the pellets that are more expensive – rather than filling a bowl full of cheaper nuggets and getting through them quickly, you'll probably find that feeding just a handful of quality nuggets will save you money in the long run.

Hay:

Hay is the most important part of a guinea pig's diet, and should make up the vast majority of their daily food intake. It helps keep their constantly growing teeth at a healthy length, as well as keeping their stomach constantly moving as they eat throughout the day and night. There are lots of different types of hay, and this will vary between countries and regions.

You can't really go wrong with hay if it is dust extracted, of which most is in the UK and you will often see labelled on packaging. Guinea pigs aren't usually fussy about types of hay either and will happily eat whichever they get.

However, if you're still stuck on which to buy and want to make sure they're getting the best, or even tips on cost effective ways to buy hay, then continue reading.

Most guinea pig owners are surprised to find how much hay their guinea pigs get through, and so keeping cost down can be a key factor in which to buy in order to make sure they have an abundance of it. The best option for this is to bulk buy hay from local farms or animal feed shops. It's cheaper because it hasn't come far, and of course you're buying a lot in one go. A drawback to this, for some, is storing the hay. It needs to breathe, but stay dry, so make sure you have the right environment for this if bulk buying is something you decide to do.

If you don't have the space, then you should find lots of variety from your local pet store; I even bought a bag from a supermarket recently which I was pleasantly surprised by. If travelling is an issue for you, you can even order hay subscriptions online and get a set amount delivered to your door. These subscriptions can be pricier, but I find it is often the greenest and sweetest hay and can save you a car journey if you struggle for time.

Fruit and Vegetables:

How much do they need and what are the best fruit and vegetables to feed them?

This is something that even the most experienced owners of guinea pigs are still debating in so many guinea pig forums, and there never really seems to be one final answer. So, I'm going to put it straight once and for all.

Why do guinea pigs even need vegetables?

Guinea pigs, like humans, need to consume vitamin C, as their body doesn't produce or store it on its own. In fact, they need roughly 10–30mg per day (www.azeah.com/guinea-pigs/vitamin-c-recommendations-guinea-pigs). To put that into perspective, that's about ½ a medium orange to me and you; but what should guinea pigs eat?

There are lots of fruit and veg that contain vitamin C, from oranges and guava to parsley and pepper, however, this does not mean there is one all-round food that should be fed every day. In fact, as much as these are high in vitamin C, they also have things in them that too much of can have a negative effect on your guinea pig's health. If you were to feed a guinea pig enough fresh orange daily to fulfil their vitamin C requirements, for example, the high level of sugar and acidity could lead to mouth sores and other problems. The occasional slice of orange, on the other hand, would go down a treat and be beneficial to them.

If you're looking for the simple, fast answer, then it's to simply offer a *variety*. Approximately 1 cup per guinea pig, per day. But it's a good idea to know what and why we don't feed certain things too often. Once you know this, it'll be easy, and when you buy some fruit and veg you haven't had in a while for your own meals, keep this book on hand to check if it's safe and your guinea pigs will love the variety that comes from feeding scraps from your own meals – we should be eating a variety too, of course.

Safe vs Unsafe Fruit, Vegetables and Food Chart

Safe Fruit and Vegetables	Unsafe Food
Asparagus	Potato and potato tops
Basil	Rhubarb (including the leaves)
Bok Choy	Tomato leaves
Broccoli	Chocolate
Brussel Sprouts	Sweets
Cabbage	Caffeine
Carrots and carrot tops	Onions
Cauliflower (including leaves and stalks)	Garlic
Celery	Mushrooms
Chicory	Iceberg lettuce
Coriander	Avocados
Courgette	Nuts
Cucumber	Seeds
Dandelion (flower and leaf)	Corn kernels
Dill	Peanut butter
Kale	Dairy

Parsley	Bread
Parsnip	Meat
Radish	
Red cabbage	
Romaine lettuce (any lettuce variety except iceberg lettuce)	
Rocket	
Salad peppers (the whole thing, including the seeds)	
Savoy cabbage	
Spinach	
Turnips	
Tomato (including the seeds, but not the stem and leaves)	
Watercress	

Some great resources for diet areguinealynx.info and azeah.com/guineapigs where you'll find a food list that also shows how high in vitamin C each fruit and vegetable are. The mg of vitamin C in each vegetable do differ and it seems to be difficult to pinpoint an exact quantity of vitamin C in any vegetable; another reason why I don't think anyone should get too hung up on exact quantities, but it does give you a good idea. It's a great way to see how simply feeding the same vegetable all of the time wouldn't be as beneficial as a variety.

A common question amongst guinea pig owners is, 'Is it safe to feed [insert fruit or veg] every day?'

Variety is key, however, there are 2 things that are high in vitamin C and have little to no downsides for guinea pigs: bell peppers and grass. Every week on my shopping list are bell peppers (and yes, it is safe to feed the whole thing, seeds and all!), and in summer you'll find me picking long fresh grass most days. Then, as I'm cooking for myself, I'll chop up a little courgette one day, maybe some broccoli another, then grab a few leaves of lettuce while I'm adding salad to my sandwich before I go to work.

Don't worry if it's a little more than a cup one day, or a little less another day. If you're feeding them a variety of safe veg and their coat is healthy, then you've got it sorted. I mean, do you really pay as much attention to your own diet? Probably not, and neither do I!

Want to check something but it's not on either list? If you're not 100% sure it's safe, it's probably not worth the risk. However, trustworthy sources are PDSA, RSPCA and Guinea Pig Welfare Association.

Grass and wild plants

Grass can also form an excellent part of a guinea pig's fresh diet. There are plenty of weeds growing in a typical British garden that are safe and nutritious for guinea pigs. During certain months of the year, I often feed wild forage along with some salad pepper, and ditch the rest of the veggies from my shopping list. This saves money and the guinea pigs receive the benefits of such a variety of food that is fresher than store bought. It can be tricky to find the nutritional value of such plants, and that's why I always feed with a vegetable I know is high in vitamin C, just to make sure.

With wild plants, it's important to consider whether they are safe from things like dog/cat/fox urine, chemicals such as slug repellents and other nasties.

There are so many plants out there that guinea pigs can eat, but equally some they can't. For more information on this, I recommend reading the brilliant book *Forage & Medicinal Wild Plants: for rabbits and guinea pigs* by Helen Knutton-Allcroft. It's full of information on all of the benefits and how to correctly identify them.

Alfalfa or not?

Alfalfa (otherwise known as lucerne) is highly nutritious for pregnant, nursing, unwell or young (under 6 months old) guinea pigs. It contains too much calcium to form a large part of the average adult guinea pig's diet, and therefore it is fine in small quantities, but generally avoided.

Can you change their food any time?

Guinea pigs are pretty hardy when it comes to a change of pellets or a different brand of hay. There is certainly no harm in phasing between pellets to be on the safe side. When you pick up your guinea pigs, ask their guardian what they're currently on and you'll usually be able to take some of their current food with you so that you can add a little into what you have bought them. With vegetables, because of their water content, you will want to build this up gradually if you have guinea pigs that have not been given vegetables before.

Can guinea pigs have treats?

Yes, they can, however, be careful of many of the processed treats you can buy in pet shops. They're costly and often contain a lot of ingredients that shouldn't be part of a guinea pig's diet at all, such as eggs, seeds and nuts.

Whilst these treats aren't necessarily poisonous, they're not healthy and you'll save yourself a small fortune (and at least the price of this book) by simply taking treats off your shopping list.

Treats for guinea pigs are things like a slice of fruit, some ReadiGrass or forage mix, or a dandelion leaf or two. Not only will your guinea pig love these, but they're healthy too.

What NOT to feed your guinea pigs

This could of course be an endless list, but here are some of the common ones that are easy to get wrong:

- Unsafe fruit and vegetables (such as iceberg lettuce!)
- Dusty hay
- Muesli mixes
- Alfalfa (unless under 6 months, unwell, pregnant or nursing)
- Processed treats
- Anything you're not sure is safe to feed

Chapter Summary

Guinea pigs love to eat and it's something you'll form a bond over as they learn to see you as the provider of their favourite thing (unfortunately you will just have to accept you'll never be quite as good as a juicy piece of yellow pepper, though you'll hopefully be a close second). But as mentioned in this chapter, it's not always as straightforward as going to the pet shop and taking anything labelled suitable for guinea pigs.

But rest assured, guinea pigs' greediness will likely wind up in them eating something they shouldn't at some point – mine have nibbled the rubber on the dustpan and brush the second I've popped out of the room whilst cleaning them, and they chase after the biodegradable bags I used for their rubbish. You might find after having read this chapter that you've purchased some unsafe food from the pet shop or have been feeding too much lettuce rather than the high vitamin C foods.

Stick with the simple checklist below and the safe and unsafe chart on page 23 and you'll be sure to put them on the road to being as happy and healthy as can be.

Daily food checklist (per guinea pig per day):

- Small handful of dried guinea pig pellets
- Unlimited dust free hay
- 1 cup fresh veg
- Unlimited fresh water

Top tip: Don't get too caught up in measurements! Unlimited hay and water are the most important things and those don't need measuring.

If you've found this helpful but you're looking for a more extensive safe fruit and vegetable list, or would like to see what brands of pellets I recommend and what my piggies are currently eating, then head to www.littlecrittercare.co.uk/freegift for even more help with your piggie's diet.

CHAPTER 4
Housing Your Guinea Pigs

How big should their space be?

This *should* be as simple as popping to the local pet shop and seeing what's on offer for guinea pigs and choosing something appropriate to the space you have and your budget. Sadly, most pet shops don't sell enclosures that meet the recommended minimum size of 120cm x 60cm (or 7200cm ^{2}) for 1 or 2 guinea pigs.

Why is space important?

Housing guinea pigs in cages too small for them will not only make for unhappy guinea pigs, but you'll also have to clean them out much more often (and in turn they'll smell sooner), you won't have space to fit in the enrichment they need, they will be more likely to fall out with their cage mate resulting in you needing to buy an extra cage, and they won't be able to exercise to keep fit and healthy which could result in pricey vet bills.

Guinea pigs love to explore and they need to exercise to keep themselves fit and healthy. When guinea pigs are happy, they'll popcorn (an involuntary jump of excitement) into the air, and young guinea pigs will zoom around their cage with happiness; this is one of the joys of owning guinea pigs that everyone wants to experience, and you'll get the most out of it by providing them with lots of space!

Cage size chart

This chart shows the bare minimum cage sizes along with the recommended and preferred cage sizes depending on the amount of guinea pigs you have. These sizes are widely recognised by rescues, guinea pig forums and guinea pig experts across the UK. It is always recommended with groups of males to go up a size to prevent squabbling, e.g. if you have 2 males, go for at least the minimum recommended for 3 females.

Number of guinea pigs	Minimum cage size	Recommended cage size
1 or 2	3 x 2 C&C (cubes & correx) cage, 105cm x 70cm (or 7,350cm² / 8ft²)	4 x 2 C&C cage, 140cm x 70cm (9,800cm² / 10.5ft²)
3	4 x 2 C&C cage, 140cm x 70cm (9,800cm² / 10.5ft²)	5 x 2 C&C cage, 175 x 70cm (12,250cm² / 13ft²)
4	5 x 2 C&C cage, 175 x 70cm (12,250cm² / 13ft²)	6 x 2 C&C cage, 210 x 70cm (14,700cm² / 16ft²)
5	6 x 2 C&C cage, 210 x 70cm (14,700cm² / 16ft²)	7x 2 C&C cage, 245 x 70cm (17,150cm² / 19ft²)

And if you get really addicted to collecting guinea pigs, then as a rule, add an extra 2450cm² or 2.5 square feet per pig, which is approximately an extra 1 x 2 grids to a C&C cage.

Cage shapes and sizes vary, but it's the area of space your guinea pigs have that is the most important, providing the space isn't too narrow for them to run around in.

To work out how many square centimeters your current cage is, simply multiply the length in cm by the width in cm. If using inches, you're best to search for a square feet converter on Google.

I would personally always recommend going for the recommended cage size or bigger, especially before you take home guinea pigs as they might be young and active and really benefit from the space. It'll also help keep the smell down by having more space. The smaller the space = the more regular cleaning. However, if you only have space for the minimum cage size, that's also fine and far bigger than your average store-bought cage or hutch.

Multiple levels or not?

Guinea pigs can have multiple levels; however, this is always in addition to the minimum space on 1 level. The benefits are that it's a great way to add on space that you might not have horizontally, however, the downsides might be that guinea pigs don't always like to use ramps (the more gradual the better), they can be unsafe so make sure they have sides, and sometimes boars might feel territorial over a particular level. When I just got my guinea pigs I had an extra level, I found it a bit of a pain to get to the part underneath it to clean, and when I eventually had more space, I took that level and joined it to the end of the base of their cage and I found this much more beneficial to me and the guinea pigs. Many people make multiple levels work and they can be a brilliant additional space in garden sheds to make the most of the space.

If you've just found out they need a lot more space than you originally thought, the next chapter will talk about *where* this enclosure might go so that you can make the most of the space you have.

Should they be kept outdoors or indoors?

When I was a secondary school teacher, I'd heard lots of stories about students' pets over the years. When they're getting a new puppy, how they woke up one morning to 8 hamsters in a cage instead of 1, and even tears at the loss of their beloved companions. One story reminded me why I will never keep my guinea pigs outside in a hutch.

With the small A level art class quietly painting away, the topic of pets came up. One of the students recalled a horror story of the morning she woke up to go and feed her guinea pigs, only to find her two guinea pigs frozen to death. They had, completely accidentally, forgotten to put the cover over the hutch the night before on a cold winter's night in the UK.

Mistakes can, and will, happen. You might forget to top up their hay one morning, or have a delay on an order of wood shavings. I've made the dreaded mistake of leaving my hamster cage lid unlocked, which resulted in my hamster having a few fun hours running around the whole place, and after getting into the seeds and nuts in the kitchen, was soon found and put back into her enclosure, despite doing everything I could think of to make her enclosure escape proof.

As humans we are bound to make the odd mistake and we can't always change them once it's done. However, what we *can* do is find ways to prevent these things and make sure they're as safe as they possibly can be.

Guinea pigs must be safe from extremely cold or hot temperatures, and safe from predators. Depending on where you are in the world, this might vary, and therefore it is always a good idea to consider your own climate.

In the UK foxes are known for being able to slip latches open, fight their way into chicken wire and dig under runs.

Birds are also a concern, which is why even supervised time outside can result in a guinea pig being snatched.

Even the friendly local cat is a predator and a reason why allowing guinea pigs to play on the grass in your garden should be properly considered, planned out and supervised.

I have never understood the idea of allowing rabbits, guinea pigs, chickens, etc. to be on the grass during the day, even in a relatively secure enclosure, only to bring them into a secure enclosure at night. If you live in the UK you will know how brazen foxes can be, so don't believe that if they can get in at night they can't during the day.

As a rule, if it's not safe at night, it's not safe during the day. You may think because you're in the house you will be able to keep an eye and listen out for anything going on, but I wouldn't want to be one of the people I have heard who have had to kick a fox out of the way whilst it had hold of their bunny's foot (fortunately said bunny was fine in the end).

I recommend always keeping your guinea pigs either indoors in a home or in an outhouse such as a shed or garage. If using a garage, carefully consider whether there will be exposure to fumes or other toxins. This is not only to ensure safety from predators, but also to provide protection from the freezing temperatures in the UK along with our heatwaves as metal garage doors provide extreme heat. For colder months, you can absolutely fill their bed with hay so that they can tunnel inside to keep warm.

What type of cage or hutch should they have?

There are plenty of simple solutions to providing your guinea pigs with enough space, from ready-made hutches and cages to DIYs on a budget.

My guinea pigs live in a very different enclosure to what I knew as a child, which was a hutch outside, possibly with a run during the day. My piggies are inside where they have a consistent temperature, where I don't have to worry about the weather, and where they're a part of my home life and family. They'd be in the living room if I had my way, but of course we have to make compromises especially when sharing our space or renting a home, for example. I plan to rescue more in the future and know that this will probably only be possible in an outhouse. More guinea pigs = more poo.

Guinea pigs should be safe, free from harsh weather, and secure. You'll need to consider the weather and temperature, space, and whether you have any other pets around they'll need protection from.

Have other pets?

If you have other pets (as mentioned on page 12), consider keeping them in a room or area that your other pets cannot access, and/or make sure it has a secure lid. Personally, I would advise having a lid even if they were to be kept in a separate room; I've heard multiple horror stories of doors accidentally being left open and I wouldn't want to chance it.

Do guinea pigs jump?

Guinea pigs aren't jumpers or climbers, so if they're in a safe room or outhouse, you don't need to worry about having high sides. 30cm in height will keep most guinea pigs contained nicely. However, if keeping a boar next to a sow, their determination to get over will see them getting over this which could result in a pregnant sow. Therefore, it's sometimes worth considering something with more height e.g. 60cm and above, or something with a lid.

Should the cage be on the floor or on the ground?

Being at waist level is always preferred, not only for ease of cleaning, but you will be approaching them at your level, which can really help with taming your guinea pigs as explained in Chapter 8.) However, having them on the floor is also absolutely fine and sometimes the only solution with a large enclosure. I have had both and personally find them at waist height easier for me and it also means I can use the underneath for storage (or in my case, one of my hamsters currently lives underneath).

What materials are best?

Wood – It's strong, sturdy, and can be cut to size if making a DIY enclosure. Guinea pigs aren't nibblers like rabbits and hamsters, though some can be. They won't chew through a wooden enclosure like a hamster would, so they won't escape from it. Since wood is porous, consider how you will keep this clean and make sure you have an absorbent bedding on top. Another downside is that it can be heavy to move and isn't easily transported as temporary accommodation.

Correx or plastic – Many people use correx for the base of their guinea pig enclosure, which is a firm, easy to manipulate floor protector made from plastic. Guinea pigs might chew plastic, though, which could be dangerous, but you can buy 'nibble guards' to prevent this. This is available in many hardware stores, or you can even buy it online pre-cut specifically for your guinea pig enclosure. It's lightweight and easy to collapse and extend as you wish (if you've got the guinea pig bug, like me, you'll know how important it is to make room for more!).

Ventilation – Wire mesh or wire bars are ideal. They can't chew out and it'll provide plenty of air flow, so make sure at least 1 side of your enclosure has this air flow. You might even find you don't need either if you have a completely open top to your enclosure in a safe room or outhouse. When ventilating an outhouse, consider whether a predator might be able to get in through a window, and you could always add window grates for security.

NB: wire should never be used as flooring, that can damage guinea pig's feet, so always have a solid floor that is easy to clean.

Popular, affordable enclosures:

C&C cages are very popular for indoor guinea pig housing. C&C stands for 'cubes and correx' which are actually designed as storage solutions. These wire cubes can be adjusted to any size or shape. It's somewhat DIY but is extremely easy to put together and doesn't require any DIY skills. You won't find these at pet stores, they'll usually be at large home decorating stores though they can be difficult to find in the UK and are easier to buy online. You can even make them multiple levels. All you need are the grids, connectors and cable ties to keep them securely together (for a single level you don't even need the connectors, just cable ties and grids will do). The correx is what is used as the base. Some people skip this altogether and come up with their own solution, otherwise you can buy this pre-cut from online guinea pig cage stores, or you can buy a sheet or two from a hardware store, usually sold as a floor protector, and cut it to size yourself. This can have as much height to it as you like, but just needs to be enough to keep in the mess; most people have these approximately 15cm high. Otherwise, for the easiest solution, you can buy an all-in-one cage kit rom online guinea pig stores such as www.candcguineapigcages.co.uk which are available throughout the UK and Europe.

NB: guinea pigs 6 months or under have been known to get their heads caught in C&C grids. This can be prevented by overlapping grids to make the holes smaller, or making the sides higher (23cm minimum) with correx or cardboard.

Hutches and runs:

There is a selection of hutches available that are appropriate sizes. But please remember it is not advisable to keep hutches completely outdoors, a safe outhouse is always better, and they must always be in the shade and protected from weather extremes. A hutch itself can make a great enclosure and is very convenient to purchase. They are more costly than C&Cs but could save you space in your house. In an outhouse you could even have an enclosed run permanently attached without worrying about predators.

DIY cages:

Some people make their own enclosures completely from scratch. Sheets of wood and even Plexiglas sides to allow your guinea pigs to be more visible. You can find lots of inspiration online and use this book as a guide to check it's appropriate.

When designing and making a DIY cage, remember to consider the following:

- Will my guinea pigs have enough space?
- Will they be able to get out?
- Will anything else be able to get in?
- How will I clean the cage?
- Are the materials safe?
- Is there enough ventilation?
- Is it appropriate for the weather throughout the year?

As long as your guinea pigs' needs are met, they won't mind what kind of cage they have. It's simply about getting the most out of the space and budget you have. If guinea pigs are going to be in your home too, you might want their enclosure to fit in with your aesthetic, and that's absolutely fine.

What bedding should I use?

Bedding; my least favourite topic! But with guinea pigs being the little poo and wee machines they are, it is such an important one, and one I've had my battles with.

There are lots to choose from and they all have their pros and cons. From wood shavings flying around a room to fleece bedding needing cleaning regularly.

Finding the right type of bedding is a battle amongst many owners, and I even see arguments in guinea pig forums about this, with many being set in their ways insisting there is only one correct option (and most of these owners have only tried that one thing). Well, I've literally tried them all, and I'm going to give you the lowdown so that you can decide for yourself.

Bedding is designed to soak up urine, keep smells at bay, and at the same time keep guinea pigs dry and comfortable. As long as it does this, your guinea pigs will not care less which you go for. So, this chapter is for you, the guinea pig slave, who is going to spend at least an entire 24 hours per year cleaning out just 2 guinea pigs.

Here is a chart to help you decide which bedding might be for you (all beddings have been tried and tested by myself and my piggies):

Bedding type	Pros	Cons
Wood shavings (not the same as sawdust, which is much finer and should never be used, can be found in pet shops and equine stores)	Easily available, cheap (especially when bought in bulk), absorbent, fresh smelling, requires a weekly clean only.	Can be dusty, can contain harmful phenols (no cedar, and pine must be kiln dried), can be messy if kicked around, a regular expense, creates waste.
Paper-based bedding (a soft paper-based flake/mulch found in pet shops as well as online and some equine stores)	Easily available, safe and natural, absorbent, requires a weekly clean only.	Expensive (unless buying a bale designed for horses), can be dusty, can have a funny smell, can be messy if kicked around, a regular expense, creates waste.
Ready-made fleece liners (an absorbent layer sandwiched between wicked fleece designed to allow urine to seep through the fleece and into the absorbent layer)	One-off cost, reusable, zero dust, easy to sweep, machine washable, absorbent layer in the middle and dry on top.	Expensive initial cost, buy online or at a pet show, wear and tear on washing machine, requires regular spot cleaning, difficult to get hay out of, shouldn't be used outside.
Towel and fleece (a DIY version of a fleece liner with no sewing together of the layers)	Affordable one-off cost, easily available, zero dust, reusable, machine washable, absorbent layer in the middle and dry on top.	Layers sometimes move and can be difficult to sweep, wear and tear on washing machine, requires regular spot cleaning, difficult to get hay out of, shouldn't be used outside.
Newspaper and hay (layers of newspaper laid down, covered by a layer of hay to allow urine to pass through)	Cheap, easily available, economical reuse of paper, zero dust (only from hay).	Not very absorbent, can be expensive depending on the hay, requires regular cleaning to keep top dry, ink shouldn't be chewed and eaten.

I've tried different types and brands of bedding over the years, and still change it up depending on what's going on in my life, and what's available. If I'm away and have someone else looking after my guinea pigs, I like them to have something that only needs to be cleaned weekly, however, if I have a guinea pig that's had respiratory problems, I'll switch to newspaper and hay, or fleece liners to steer clear of any dust to be on the safe side.

Guinea pigs don't generally mind what bedding they have, though one thing I have found is that they love piles of hay.

If opting for fleece liners, you might find that piling on the hay causes a lot of work for you to remove which leads to using a hay rack. Hay racks have been known to get guinea pigs heads caught in, so be very careful when purchasing them and look at reviews before you buy. Some say that they also make hay too difficult to get to. I'm not entirely against hay racks and do believe there is a place for them, but you might find at times it necessarily to make hay as easily accessible as possible, for example a sick guinea pig that needs encouragement to eat, or you just want them to have fun playing in the piles of hay. Some people don't mind the extra effort to remove the hay from fleece which is also absolutely fine. I've found with a busy life teaching full time and running Little Critter Care, I want whichever is easier and quicker to manage whilst keeping the pigs happy, so something that requires only a weekly clean or so works for me.

Do you have to choose just one type of bedding?

I often opt for half fleece liner and half wood shavings; it means I can pile on the hay in the wood shavings zone (which becomes a bit like a giant litter tray), and use the fleece side to keep their favourite fleece cosies which they love to sleep in. When it comes to cleaning it's a quick sweep of the fleece every couple of days, and a change of shavings once or twice a week. A pet safe disinfectant is handy for a quick spray and wipe down of the cage, bowls and water bottles to keep germs at bay; I highlight recommend choosing a cruelty free brand as, sadly, there are brands that test on animals including guinea pigs.

If you're still not sure, why not try out some different wood shavings or paper bedding first, then try some old towels and a piece of wicked fleece over the top to see how you like it. Then you can see if fleece liners might be worth investing in.

It's also important to remember that brands vary too, and whilst you might not like one brand of shavings or fleece liner, it doesn't mean another won't be a perfect fit.

Just remember, as much as some people will say they have the perfect cleaning routine and they love it, it's still cleaning, and nobody wants to do it at the end of the day. But it must be done, so whatever makes it easier is always a result and your guinea pigs will love their clean cage and time to spend with you, so go for what works best for *you*.

What should I put in their cage?

With the array of guinea pig items to buy in pet shops, you might find yourself with a huge number of things in your shopping basket. Well, I'm about to tell you what you really need, and what you're probably better off saving your money on.

Constant access to hay and water is a must, so make sure there is enough to keep them going while you're out at work and overnight – you might be surprised at how quickly they eat hay!

A 500ml water bottle should suffice for 2 guinea pigs. You will want to change the water daily, so there isn't much benefit to buying a large one. For pairs of boys, you might want to buy a spare so that there is less to argue over.

There is no need for a hay rack, as they will happily pull it all out to wee on anyway, much to your annoyance. Although there are some ways you can keep the mess of hay under control, which I'll talk more about in Chapter 7. You're fine just to put the hay on top of whatever substrate you have down for them; and yes, they will poo and wee on it, but if enough is there they will weed out the best pieces. There will always be some hay 'waste' on the floor. It is a natural texture they are safe and happy to be on, so it's never really wasted.

I would also give the cute food bowls a miss! They will need a daily portion of their pellets, but they won't necessarily need to eat from a bowl, especially as you will find they often knock over their bowl trying to climb into it being the greedy piggies they are. You may want a bowl spare for water just in case of emergencies (e.g. water bottle breaking).

Places to hide are important, and these can come in many forms. If you're on a budget a simple cardboard box with some guinea pig sized holes ripped out make an excellent, free hideaway – just be careful of sellotape and that there was nothing toxic inside. You want your guinea pigs to be able to nibble on the box safely. A simple drape of fabric over one side of the enclosure can make a lovely dark area without taking up space in the cage. You can also buy fabric beds which guinea pigs love to lie on and they can come in all colours, shapes and patterns. Consider that they will wee where they relax, so you will need to wash these in the washing machine, which may not be ideal for everyone.

Top money saving tip: avoid any tubes or tunnels that can't go in the wash or be wiped clean – once they start pooing and weeing in a natural straw tube it is a nightmare to clean and will only end up in the bin.

I have a mixture of hideaways I've collected over the years; some were a waste of money and some of the cheapest options are the guinea pigs' favourites. Most importantly, make sure each pig has a separate place to hide as they won't always want to be right next to one another.

For outdoor guinea pigs, please see Chapter 4 for some extra items you might want to add for particularly warm or cold weather.

That's really all there is to it. When I say basic needs, I really mean everything they need to be completely happy and content. There are a few things you can do to make their space more exciting for them, but for now…

Here's your essential guide for filling the cage with everything they need:

- Bedding
- Water bottle or bowl
- Lots of hay
- Scattered food (no need for a bowl)
- 1 place to hide per pig

There's nothing wrong with buying extra things at all, provided they're safe. You'll of course want to change their hideaways up a little as they get dirty and have spares. However, this book isn't 'How to provide the most expensive and luxury care for your guinea pigs', it's a simple guide that will allow you to take the best care of your guinea pigs even if you're on a budget. Of course, if you want to buy cute hideaways that cost a little more, or a bowl with your guinea pigs name on it, go for it! The piggies will still be happy either way and that's all that matters. But if you want to make sure you're providing some extra enrichment for them then continue reading…

How do I keep them entertained?

Guinea pigs are simple creatures in this respect, and love nothing more than the company of their own kind and a big pile of hay to play around in.

You want to free up enough space that they have some clear space to run around and do zoomies, and enough comfortable places to sit and graze on hay.

You'll often find that buying toys from pet stores will be a complete waste of money, while they ignore them and continue to wander around trying to find the best pieces of hay. In fact, some of these toys can be dangerous; I've heard countless stories of guinea pigs getting their head stuck in small hay racks, or digesting unsafe 'edible' toys. Always do your research on something for your guinea pig before you buy it and don't be tricked by the 'safe for guinea pigs' label.

A great way to encourage some healthy activity is by scatter feeding their food, rather than presenting it in a bowl in order to encourage natural foraging. You can also do this with sweeter, treat hays such as ReadiGrass, or natural forage mixes of dried flowers and herbs. Sprinkle food around their enclosure and they will be busy searching for their favourite pieces.

Do they need time outside of their cage?

It is very common to be advised to allow guineas pigs out for exercise for a certain amount of time each day. My theory on this is that because most pet shops sell cages that are way too small, or that are outside connected to a larger run, it became the 'done' thing to advise owners to make sure they get out of the hutch each day. This of course would benefit the guinea pigs massively, however, what really should be the case is that they should be in suitable housing 24/7.

So, if your guinea pigs have a large enclosure, meeting at least the minimum recommended size (see Chapter 4) or even larger, then they don't *need* to have daily time outside their enclosure. Would your guinea pigs still enjoy exploring a different environment? Of course.

Time outside in a safe and secure run during pleasant weather to graze on grass, or inside in a play pen or safe room is an exciting new surrounding for your guinea pigs to explore. Make sure they have places to hide, and some hay and water to access when they need. Remember that they will still wee and poo, so a floor that is easy to wipe, or placing something absorbent down like towels or fleece liners will help protect your carpet.

Do you need to supervise them all the time?

If they're indoors in a secure playpen with everything they need just like their safe cage set-up, you could happily leave them to it. However, if they have access to anything that might be dangerous such as wires, holes they might get their head stuck in, or places you don't want them to mess on, then yes you must supervise them to make sure they are safe. C&C grids or a playpen can be great for containing them or blocking off areas of the room you don't want them to get to. If outdoors, please see Chapter 4 where I talk all about outdoor guinea pigs.

NB: guinea pigs are sensitive to changes in temperature, so if they live outside where it is chilly, and you then bring them into a warm house in winter, this isn't advised. Equally bringing them from a warm house to cold outside temperatures isn't a good idea either. You might see your neighbour's piggies doing fine in their run on a chilly afternoon when they already live outside, but if yours have been indoors all winter your guinea pigs won't necessarily do well with chilly weather outdoors.

Chapter summary

Well, if from reading this chapter I've saved you from buying the typical cage or hutch you'll find in your local pet shop that is way too small (and also quite expensive for its size) then my mission to happier guinea pigs is well on its way! If you want your guinea pigs to have a better chance of getting along and even clean them out less frequently then space is the way to go. If you have a great pet shop that provides the minimum recommended cage size then get in touch with me as I'd love to make these enclosures even easier for people to find.

Your guinea pig's favourite things to do will be to hide, sleep, eat and poo. And as much as I know how tempting it will be to treat your guinea pigs to some of the tonnes of toys and treats available in pet stores, they'll never appreciate them as much as they will a simple cardboard box and a big pile of hay.

So, before you stock your cart up with an array of pricey toys and brightly packaged treats, check out the list below for what you really need for your guinea pigs (then pop your spare cash into a worry-free vet fund for later).

Your essential-8 shopping list for a pair of happy, healthy guinea pigs:

- A large enclosure over 1 level (recommended minimum 9,000cm^2, with additional levels counting as extra space)
- A space for their enclosure that is safe from weather extremes and predators
- A safe and absorbent bedding
- Places to hide per guinea pig
- LOTS of hay
- A bag of healthy pellets
- Fresh vegetables
- 500ml water bottle
- Cruelty free pet-safe disinfectant

Top tip: remember to scrap the food bowls and hay racks if you can. Piles of hay and scattering their pellets and veg will encourage natural exercise.

It's really important you have this all ready and set up before getting your guinea pigs. In the next chapter, I'll be talking all about how to prepare for the exciting moment you take your new guinea pig/s home!

CHAPTER 5
Bringing Your Guinea Pigs Home

So, you've got this far into the book and you've decided to bring home a pair (or more) of guinea pigs. Congratulations! This is super exciting, and I know that having read this book so far, you'll make a great piggie parent.

Travelling to a new environment can be a stressful time for guinea pigs, from the car journey to the new sounds, sights and smells of a different place.

And I know you'll want them to feel as comfortable and settled as possible.

In this chapter you'll find out what you need to know to make bringing your guinea pigs home a stress-free and simple process in 3 simple steps.

Step 1 – Set up the enclosure before the pigs come home.

Before you travel home with your guinea pigs, which I'll tell you how to do in step 2, you will want to have their cage and supplies all ready for them so that you can pop them in straight after their journey. This also gives you time to iron out any problems you might've come across.

Something I mention a lot in Chapter 8 and to my clients, is having hideaways that aren't too 'closed in'. I think this is particularly important when you first bring your guinea pigs home since not only will you be able to catch a glimpse at them to check they're OK, but they'll learn quickly that there is nothing to be afraid of. A simple cardboard box with multiple holes works perfectly. I honestly can't stress enough how underrated this trick is. You see, if you give them hideaways that have 1 hole that they can completely hide away in, they will hide and hear frightening unknown noises.

Imagine being in a tent at night with a rustle in the woods… it's just a hedgehog, but whilst you stay in your tent you start to imagine all sorts of ghastly beasts, however, when you peer outside your tent and see that hedgehog, you can immediately relax! So, imagine how your guinea pigs feel when they're hiding away in their tunnel, too afraid to look out. You can gently encourage them to observe by providing shelter but also allowing them to see what's going on.

Not only are multiple openings good for building up their confidence, but it can stop any bickering between your guinea pigs by allowing the other to run away when needed. It really is a win–win.

In order to make sure you and your guinea pigs are stress-free, go through the checklist in Chapter 4 and make sure you've got everything your guinea pigs need, ready and set up, to go straight into their new home when they arrive.

Step 2 – Travel safely with your guinea pigs

My once unplanned travel home with my first hamster, Trev, resulted in him biting me through his travel box, only to arrive home just in the nick of time before an escape. I'd read all of the information on how to keep hamsters, but for some reason hadn't thought too much into how I might take him home, especially when I'd seen so many people take theirs home in small cardboard boxes.

Guinea pigs aren't ones for escaping, but travelling can be a scary experience for them, whether you're walking on a very short journey, or in a car or even public transport. Your job is to keep them as comfortable as possible on this journey.

Firstly, have a safe carrier for them. Now, guinea pigs are probably one of the few rodents you could get away with a cardboard box not being chewed, though I like to use a well-ventilated cat carrier either made from plastic or a strong fabric. Some of the carriers designed for guinea pigs are fine for baby guinea pigs but not so much as they grow older. You don't want this carrier to be too big that they can move around too much in case of an accident, but equally you want enough space to fit them nicely without being on top of one another.

Depending on how long your journey is, you will want to have some essentials in their carrier for them. Newspaper, hay and fresh veg are perfect for short or long journeys. A water bottle is difficult to manage whilst transporting, so fresh veg can act as hydration for them and hay to keep their guts moving. Newspaper will help soak up their urine, but prepare for them to run underneath the newspaper and completely mess up this set-up – not to worry. If it's a particularly long journey over a number of hours then consider having breaks from movement so that they can relax and eat or drink from a bowl or bottle.

It is quite normal for guinea pigs to be too frightened to eat on journeys, though if you can hear them nibbling then they're quite content.

If you're in a car, use the seat belts to strap their carrier in as best as you can, and consider having someone with you to keep an eye on them in the back seat.

Consider what you might come across on your journey: are there dogs around that might come up close? Is there a cold breeze they need protecting from? Is it a hot day where you might need air con and better ventilation? Think of how you can avoid and minimise these situations as much as possible. I read recently in a guinea pig forum that someone decided to pick up their guinea pigs on a different day because there was a heatwave due, which is a simple but perfect solution.

Step 3 – Leave them alone for a couple of days

I know it can be so tempting to cuddle these adorable little critters once they're home, but just remember how over-whelmed they already are, and having this unknown giant pick them up is only going to add to that fear.

Give them at least 48 hours to settle in, without touching them. Of course, you can place your hand in to give them food, change their water and give them a spot clean if needed, but refrain from moving them from their cage or touching them just for this time at least. Guinea pigs are fast learners and the sooner they realise nothing is there to harm them, the better.

Chapter Summary

A short, but important chapter! Bringing our guinea pigs home is not something many of us think about, particularly when we're so busy making sure we know how to care for them.

Of course, sometimes, there are just those moments when you might bring a pet home impulsively; when you love animals as much as I do this happens more often than you intend to! I have even picked up an injured rabbit from the wild before and had to rummage through my car for a box which did the trick. I actually keep a pet carrier in my car just in case (a bit extreme, but I drive around a lot visiting people's pets and it's nice knowing I'm prepared for an injured animal on the road or a pet emergency). I'm sure one of these days it'll be used to help a pair of guinea pigs that just can't wait.

I am a planner, though, and I think you should be too; after all you're already reading a book all about guinea pigs in preparation for getting your first pair, or maybe you've already got them and are looking for useful tips on how to make things easier next time (and if you have guinea pigs you know there will be a next time because they're just too adorable!).

So, make sure you follow the 3 simple steps to settling in:

- Step 1 – Set up the enclosure before the pigs come home
- Step 2 – Travel safely with your guinea pigs
- Step 3 – Leave them alone for a couple of days

While you wait for them to settle in, why not read Chapter 6 where you will learn to 'squeak' guinea pig whilst you observe them. When you eventually start to handle them (Chapter 8) you'll know exactly what they like and what they don't like.

CHAPTER 6
Learn to 'Squeak' Guinea Pig

Guinea pigs are very vocal creatures and have some odd behaviours. It is quite common when first owning guinea pigs to be unsure of whether our guinea pigs are happy or not. When I first got guinea pigs, I was forever googling what each noise meant, and ended up confused as to whether my guinea pig liked or hated me. A strange noise even led me to take them to the vets on more than one occasion which wasn't necessary.

The great thing about guinea pigs is that they are such great communicators, not only to one another but to us humans too. So much so that some noises and behaviours of the domestic guinea pig have changed from those of their wild counterparts.

A lot of noises will depend on their context, and they almost always link to body language, so with any noise always pay close attention not only to the sound but to what prompted the sound and how they are behaving. This combination is the key to being a guinea pig whisperer.

Below is a list of a range of noises and body language that will help you speak guinea pig!

These noises are readily available to hear on the internet with a simple google if you're unsure of the sound, though each noise can vary in volume and between guinea pigs so all won't sound exactly the same. It can take some time to get used to, so don't worry if you don't know everything right away.

Noises

Chutting

Chutting sounds a bit like a low, quiet frog's croak. I prefer to call this more of a mumble.

It's a pleasant sound and you will usually hear it when they are exploring, and it's not unusual to hear it from multiple guinea pigs at one time.

When you hear this noise, they're basically saying:

"Oow! What's going on? What's this? This is interesting…" and just general chitter chatter.

I like to think of it as a little old lady talking to herself about something good that's happened that day!

Wheeking

This sounds like a repetitive high-pitched squeak, and one you probably hear often. It can vary in volume and once one guinea pig starts, the rest will usually follow.

It is usually accompanied by running around and will likely be triggered by the rustling of a bag or a fridge opening.

They are saying:

"I can hear food! I'm so excited! Feed me!"

You'll likely hear this daily when bringing food, cleaning out, or simply entering the room because they *think* you're bringing food. If you have new guinea pigs that are nervous, you may not hear wheeking for a while, and that is completely normal.

Although similar to a squeal, which is associated with something guinea pigs hate, this is more of a repetitive oink.

They will often know when it's dinner time if you stick to a strict routine and will definitely let you know if you've forgotten them!

Fun fact: this noise is exclusively for humans and never happens in the wild!

Rumbling

It's a deep sound similar to a purr, often accompanied by a strange waddle called 'strutting'. The noise doesn't flow like a purr, it is made up of more of an abrupt, deeper, repetitive sound similar to a machine gun.

They are saying:

"Look at how fabulous I am, I'm the best."

This is a dominant sound, often made by males, but sometimes more dominant females like my guinea pig, Onyx. This is very common with bonding, but you might even hear it daily, or sometimes more often when a female is in heat.

It's not anything to worry about, particularly if the other guinea pig is submissive and doesn't show signs of aggression in response.

It's often associated with mating and 'wooing', but either gender will do it, neutered or not, and is just a show of how great they are and that others should keep in line more than anything.

Purring

Often accompanied by a physical shudder, this purring sound is different to the low-pitched, relaxed purr of a cat. It is a little higher pitched and short.

While many say this noise can be good or bad, in my experience it is always an annoyed noise.

You will likely hear it if you stroke them near their back/bum. If they make this purring noise and you continue, they will likely get up and walk off or try and kick you off them.

This will sometimes happen and isn't the end of the world and doesn't mean your guinea pig doesn't like you, but try to listen to them and respond appropriately.

Teeth chattering

A quiet, high-pitched 'ch-ch-ch-ch-ch-ch-ch…'

This isn't a good sound, but it's not necessarily anything to worry about.

They are saying:

"I'm not sure I'm happy with this, in fact, I'm getting a little angry…"

When might you hear this noise?

- When another guinea pig is getting too close to them
- When you're stroking them somewhere they don't like
- When you're about to feed them; they're so greedy that when the excitement of you rustling the bag of fresh hay and veg is over, they might just get fed up with you taking so long and get 'hangry' (a word-blend of hungry and angry!)

It is usually not a problem as you or the other guinea pig back down. However, in a case of guinea pig introductions, it is something to watch out for. If another guinea pig teeth chatters back, both raising their heads to completely face one another, it is a sign a fight could break out. This would be a time where I might do something to divert their attention with a noise or fresh food.

Usually, guinea pigs are happy to move on and quickly get over something that might annoy them, so this is a completely normal noise during introductions or even between a well-established pair.

Complaining/whining

A high-pitched whine, or even a series of repetitive croaks similar to 'chutting' that get higher pitched towards the end of the sound. There can be quite a few different names for this. It is not to be confused with a high-pitched squeal.

This noise is usually accompanied by suddenly running away from another guinea pig, or even a little kick back or wiggle of the bum to essentially say:

"Get off me, I don't like what you're doing."

This is a completely normal noise and is nothing to interfere with or be concerned about when one guinea pig makes this noise to another.

In guinea pig introductions, this is a good noise to hear, because it isn't aggressive, it is just one guinea pig saying to another they don't like it but don't want any trouble.

When else might you hear this noise?

- when you pick them up
- when you stroke them where they don't like (usually the bum/back area)
- during nail trimming and health checks

It is a noise to avoid, but something you will likely hear and isn't at all uncommon. It can be a good way to know that you are doing something they don't like so you can adjust what you're doing.

Squeal

A high-pitched, sometimes drawn-out squeal.

They are saying:

"I hate this – stop!"

or

"Ouch!"

It is not a sound you will hear often and can be a sign of pain.

My guinea pig, Wiggy, used to do this when being brushed, even with a wide toothed comb on hair that wasn't even tangled.

I listened to this and made a few changes to his grooming routine which involved a shorter haircut (he much preferred the occasional haircut to having a more regular hair brush) and a child's detangling brush (rather than the standard pet brush you find in most pet stores) which immediately stopped him squealing!

You might hear this noise when you pick up your guinea pig, out of fear, or pain. They might even make this noise after their cage mate pushes them a little too far, and is more of an exaggerated 'whine'.

You will also likely hear this noise if you accidentally cut the quick while nail trimming, and *definitely* if they must have an injection at the vets.

Remember: guinea pigs are drama queens, and so you will hear this noise occasionally, sometimes without anything being wrong, so don't beat yourself up about it if you hear it, but do listen to it and think about the context of the squeal so that you can adjust anything to ease their discomfort. The taming process also helps a lot as they feel less fearful and are less likely to overreact.

Hooting

A low-pitched hooting from their breath, or almost like a croak from the chest.

This can either signal heart trouble or some sort of respiratory issue, or simply a bit of hay stuck.

It is something to keep an eye on. When I first heard this noise from Onyx, it soon went away, but I took her to the vets just in case it was a respiratory issue. She was fine, and I hear this noise from her fairly regularly and know that it is not a major cause for concern. If I ever hear it continuously or hear it suddenly from Luna who had never made this noise, that would be another sign for me to go for another vet visit.

Cough/sneeze

Like a baby's muffled cough or sneeze.

Much like 'hooting' it could signal a problem, or they could be trying to clear some food from their throat.

If it is a regular occurrence throughout the day and seems unusual for your guinea pig, see a vet for some clarification.

Hiccup

Sounds a bit like a burp, or even a cough/sneeze, but is accompanied by what I can only describe as what looks like your guinea pig is heaving and trying to be sick.

It is physically impossible for a guinea pig to vomit, but this really does look like the closest thing to it and can be quite scary.

Though you might be tempted if it seems like they're choking to perform some sort of guinea pig Heimlich manoeuvre – don't (it's not only dangerous, but useless). You just need to let them work it out on their own and it will be fine.

You will probably never witness this, but if you do, this will hopefully remind you not to panic. Wait it out and it will be fine!

Chirping

This sounds just like a bird chirping.

Chirping is a guinea pig sound that nobody has a definite answer for. Some say it means 'danger', whilst others question why guinea pigs would make the noise of a bird if they felt they were in real danger.

It is a very rare noise to hear and can be quite alarming, though you will likely never hear it. But if you do, don't worry, they will eventually stop and will be fine. Try placing them next to their cage mates, make sure they have places to hide to feel safe. If you think there was a genuine cause for this sudden noise, such as living outside and have a predator get close, time to think of a way to avoid this happening again and make sure they are, and *feel*, safe.

Body language

Popcorning

Popcorning is where a guinea pig will jump up in a random spasm of happiness. This is much more common in younger guinea pigs, but that doesn't mean you won't see it in older guinea pigs. When you see this, your guinea pig is so happy they can't control themselves!

Zoomies

Sometimes, particularly with younger guinea pigs, they will run fast laps of happy excitement. This is one of the reasons why it's so important to give them as much space as you can to express these behaviours at any time of day or night.

Strutting

Usually accompanied by the 'rumble' noise, is where a guinea pig will waddle, slowly moving their bums from side to side. It is a sign of dominance and very common to see. It is not aggressive at all, just showing off.

Lying down, stretched out with legs kicked back

This is the sign of a very comfortable and contented guinea pig. They feel so comfortable in their surroundings that they can happily let their guard down. If you see this, you're an awesome owner! This is also heavily influenced by the guinea pig's personality; some will just naturally have more confidence than others.

Hunching

When a guinea pig is hunched over, they're either just about to eat a poo straight from the source, or they're very unwell. If your guinea pig doesn't immediately spring out of this position, then you should arrange an appointment with the vet urgently.

Mounting

When a guinea pig tries to climb onto the back of another guinea pig, they may be trying to mate, but it is also a completely normal way of trying to assert dominance. You will see this more commonly from males, but also females do this. It is nothing to be concerned about, though of course when keeping a male and female together, either the male needs to be neutered and/or the female spayed. That is the only way besides complete separation to prevent babies.

Touching noses

When guinea pigs touch noses, it is simply a friendly greeting. Guinea pigs aren't one to cuddle up, lick or groom one another, so this is their way of acknowledging one another.

Marking territory

Guinea pigs will sometimes drag their bottoms along the ground to mark their territory. It is a very subtle move and often goes unnoticed, but is completely normal.

Head raising

When one guinea pig raises their head to another, they are telling them to watch out. Onyx often likes to rumble strut, and sometimes follow and annoy Luna. When Luna turns around and raises her head, Onyx backs down as she knows she has taken it too far. This has the potential to turn serious if Onyx were to also raise her head and refuse to back down; you then have two guinea pigs that are prepared to fight.

Fighting

When guinea pigs fight it can be very scary, but a scrabble isn't necessarily anything to worry about, especially when you're just introducing them. You can often calm things down by diverting their attention to fresh vegetables. Never put your hand in to try and separate fighting guinea pigs as you could be seriously bitten and need medication for an infection. You can, however, use something like a dustpan or oven mitt to break up the fight should it become serious. The rule of thumb is when blood is drawn, permanently separate the fighting guinea pigs.

Yawning

Usually when lying down, guinea pigs will open their mouths very widely to yawn and completely expose their teeth. This is natural and a sign of a very relaxed and comfortable guinea pig. In some cases, it might be a way of showing another guinea pig their teeth as a sign of dominance.

Chapter Summary

Now that's a lot of different noises and behaviours to take in, and you may not hear or see some of them ever. It can take a while to learn how to squeak guinea pig, but once you've cracked it, you'll become a fellow guinea pig whisperer in no time.

Guinea pig noises are so unique and what makes them such special rodents. We're able to understand them and know when they're happy, when they're not happy, and respond to them (yes, you quite literally will find yourself 'wheeking' at them). In fact, they're so good at responding to our noises you can even train them to come over for food at any noise you like.

Their noises are also a reason you might not want them in a room where you need peace and quiet, though.

If you're a new owner or have just brought home a new guinea pig and are wondering why you don't hear or see the happy behaviours such as wheeking and popcorning, don't worry. It is totally normal for your guinea pigs to be nervous at this stage and doesn't mean you're doing anything wrong. There's more about that in Chapter 8 on taming.

If you've just got a new pair, or aren't sure if your guinea pigs are getting along, there is more about this in Chapter 8 on guinea pig introductions.

Now, if you'd actually like to hear these sounds for a little more clarity, go to www.littlecrittercare.co.uk/freegift where you'll be able to listen to these noises.

CHAPTER 7
Litter Training: No Mess, Less Stress

Can guinea pigs be litter trained?

If you're envisioning a guinea pig free-roaming around your home, politely using their litter tray and hopping out in a mess-free guinea pig land, then I'm sorry to shatter your dreams... Guinea pigs are naturally messy critters, and you won't find that by simply popping a litter tray into their cage because they will naturally want to only wee in it like a hamster or rabbit does. However, by putting a few things in place, you can encourage them to urinate in the litter tray and poo in certain areas more than others, so keeping other areas cleaner.

In 2019 I wrote an eBook, *How to Potty Train Your Little Critter in 5 Days: No Mess, Less Stress* , in which I applied and simplified what I've learnt over the years with my own, and clients' little critters. The method took a few years to perfect, and I even wrote the guide for hamster and rabbit owners too. Much of this chapter is extracted from that eBook, just for guinea pigs.

Why would you want to litter train a guinea pig?

In Chapter 4, I talked about how one of the cons to using fleece liners is the problem with removing hay from them. You might even be fed up with the amount of wood shavings you have to throw away each week, or maybe you're fed up with having to wash their entire cosy because one of the guinea pigs urinated in it as soon as they entered. Wouldn't it be great if you could just clean certain areas and not have to wash the whole thing like you usually do?

If you're already happy with your cleaning routine and your guinea pigs are clean and happy, then feel free to skip this chapter.

However, if you're struggling to balance the mess created with the time and resources you have, then keep reading for your potty-training solution.

How to litter train your guinea pig in 5 days

Step 1 – Days 1–3

Firstly, find out WHERE your guinea pigs like to do their business. It may seem counterproductive to spend more time on this stage than with an actual litter tray, but I swear this is the most important part of litter training. Knowing what your pet already likes to do is going to mean that you don't need to change their behaviour. This guide is not about changing your pet's behaviour, it's going to work WITH your pet's behaviour and create a solution that makes it easier for you and your pet.

Common places to find urine will be in a certain corner of their enclosure, or in a hidden, darker area. Urine is what smells, and there will often be a cluster of poo with the urine, so look for that. Begin by observing your pets with your normal cleaning routine. Where are they leaving the most mess? Is it always where they eat? Where they sleep? Can you actually tell where they wee or do you need to try a different type of bedding to make it easier to spot, such as wood based so it's easy to pick out the yellow, damp stain?

Guinea pigs will naturally poo where they eat. They also poo where they sleep and while they're simply pottering about and typically produce a lot more mess than other rodents. There are ways to manage this and make big clean outs far less frequent for all of these small furries. You should still be able to pick out specific spots where your little critter tends to go more often – is this under a particular hideaway? Or on the hay and close by? Keep checking and try moving things around to see if it changes.

Step 2 – Day 4

So, you've found out where your pet wees and poos the most – but what next? This is where we place something to catch the toilet habits, making it super easy to remove in step 3, resulting in less need to clean the entire enclosure. Not only this, but we want to make that area an even more appealing place to do their business so that there are fewer accidents around the rest of the enclosure.

Scrap the 'guinea pig litter trays' from the pet shop and opt for a shallow cat litter box/tray, or DIY your own by buying a large tray or plastic bin from a home store with high sides and cut holes out. Guinea pigs love to eat while they poo so pile lots of hay on top after you fill the tray with a safe substrate such as wood shavings (not cedar), newspaper, or paper or wood-based pellets – never use cat litter unless it is made from wood or paper because they might eat it. Lining with newspaper can make it even easier to clean later. It is also helpful to put a small amount of their dirty litter into this tray to remind your guinea pigs that's where they should go.

Guinea pigs will likely have a number of places they will go, and as much as you try to get them to go in only one place, it is unheard of. But this is fine, because we can easily make multiple litter areas. This is why I love fleece liners, because you can place mini fleece liners just where you need them. I like to place one in each corner, and under their tunnels. Having hideaways that have an absorbent bottom is also great as these can simply be taken out when soiled without needing to wash the whole thing. Place a litter tray wherever they go most. They also like to munch on hay while they pee and poo, so make sure you put lots of hay in the tray and top up regularly to make sure they always have a fresh supply of hay. It is important to give this some time as they may simply be unsure of the new object placed in their enclosure, and not be comfortable enough to relax there yet.

Step 3 – Day 5

The next time you go to clean your little critter out, you should find that there is more mess in your litter area/s than anywhere else in the cage. If not, not to worry, just give it a little time, and even go back to step 1 as you may find you thought they went in corners but since you moved their favourite hideaway to the centre of the enclosure they keep going there. It can take a few attempts to find the perfect set up, but once you do it is going to save you so much time! With litter trays, simply scoop out the mess (only the mess, no need to change the whole thing), use a pet safe disinfectant, and top up with fresh substrate. This will occasionally require a full clean, but not half as regularly as you've been doing a full cage clean up until now.

If your guinea pigs are on fleece simply brush up the poo with a dustpan and brush, stick the soiled mini fleece pads into your washing basket, and replace with fresh pads – you may find they didn't even go in one or more of the corners, in which case, leave those fleece pads there!

Once the poo around the rest of the cage builds up to a point you can't spot clean, that's when it's time for a full cage clean. Be patient with these steps and I can assure you, you will be having to do a full cage clean far less regularly than you once were, meaning more time to spend playing and bonding with your pets!

Chapter summary

You might not need to litter train your guinea pigs if you're already happy with your cleaning routine. But if you're looking to make your routine quicker, easier and less messy, then here's a recap of the 3 steps:

Step 1 – WHERE'S THE POO AT? – Spend 3 days observing where your little critter does their business. Make notes, and see if it changes when you move things around the cage.

Step 2 – POTTY PREPARATION – Set up your potty zones to catch as much mess as possible with a litter tray and fleece liners.

Step 3 – SCOOP THE POOP – Scoop up the contained mess. Revisit step 1 if there is urine outside of your designated pee zone.

If you want more help with litter training your guinea pigs, go to www.littlecrittercare.co.uk/freegift.

CHAPTER 8
How to Become a Guinea Pig Whisperer: Taming Your Guinea Pigs

So, you've got guinea pigs, but your visions of these cute critters running to you for affection and dreams of watching Netflix all evening cuddled up with your piggies aren't quite turning out the way you hoped and all they want to do is run away from you!

This is very common at the start of guinea pig ownership, but you might even be months or years down the line still wondering when they might finally decide to like you.

Well, I'm here to tell you that you absolutely can tame your guinea pigs, though it will take some work, but you AND your piggies will be so much more confident and happier for it.

But firstly, let's start to understand what these little critters are thinking and why they are always running away.

Why do my guinea pigs run away from me?

If you've just brought your guinea pigs home, or you've only had them for a week or so, then it is completely normal for them to run away from you. How would you feel if you moved to a completely new environment, not knowing what to expect, and a giant creature walks in each day, makes noises, and occasionally tries to lift you up? Probably terrified, right? However, they should quickly start to see that the giant creature provides them with all their favourite things worth popcorning over: fresh hay, veg, and a clean space.

Maybe you've had guinea pigs for a while and still find them running away from you? Then for whatever reason, they still believe there is something to fear. It can be really frustrating as an owner, because nobody wants to feel disliked, and of course you want your guinea pigs to be happy. You might wonder how they can possibly be happy when they run away in fright from you? It's very common for people to ask why their pigs are still frightened. Often people think they should just accept it, they lose hope, and sadly some guinea pigs end up back at rescues because they're not tame enough.

Hopefully you're reading this because you want your guinea pigs to be happy to see you! And not just for your own personal gratification, but because you want them to realise there's nothing to be scared of.

What are guinea pigs scared of?

When I lived in my old place my kitchen wasn't far from their room, and every time I opened the fridge, I would hear Luna and Onyx 'wheeking', even when I was just getting myself a snack. However, this wasn't always the case. When I first brought them home, they had never been in someone's house and had probably never heard a fridge before, and when I walked into the room they would run away and hide.

They were previously in a large chain pet store up for adoption. They'd been in there some time and had probably, on numerous occasions, had someone reach in to grab them to be given to a stranger to hold in a loud and busy shop. When you put yourself in the same position, it's really no wonder they're terrified of people.

They're prey animals, so essentially, they're scared of predators. Besides a bit of a nip if they try really hard, they've got no chance for proper defence – their defence is to RUN!

This behaviour is completely natural, and this won't ever change, it's wired into them. However, you can teach them what *isn't* a threat.

Loud noises

Loud or sudden noises might signal something terrible is about to happen, especially in the wild. The first time they ever hear the rustle of a plastic bag, they will be terrified, they don't know what it is, and it could certainly signal danger, so they run and hide! However, every time they hear the rustle of a plastic bag and they receive food, they will then start to LOVE that sound.

Sudden movement

Predators move slowly, eyeing out their prey… and when they finally pounce, they must do it quickly as this is their prey's chance to get away. Guinea pigs naturally associate sudden movement or sound with a possible predator and must run to safety. Sudden movements are naturally going to occur in their environment, and so rather than try to stop it, you can teach them that sudden sounds and movements are nothing to fear.

Being picked up

One of the predators to guinea pigs are birds, who will, if given a chance, swoop from a height and pick them up with their claws. Does this sound familiar? When you go to pick up your guinea pigs, are you coming from above?

How you access the enclosure is going to be a big help in making them feel more confident and less threatened. As explained in Chapter 8, having them up at waist height will certainly help with this, and if not, being able to crouch down and approach from their level with a side entrance is a good alternative.

The unknown

All of the fears mentioned above stem down to a fear of the unknown, and if there is any sort of unusual sound, movement or touch, they will want to hide from it, just in case it is a predator.

This is why my whole taming theory is based around exposure; when we expose them to things that aren't a threat to them, that thing is no longer unusual to them and is no longer a warning or something to fear and can even be something they enjoy.

This might sound strange and counterproductive. I used to tiptoe around them, worried about frightening them, and it was my partner, Brett, who would noisily get ready for work in the spare room with the guinea pigs, opening and closing cupboards and moving around the room in a hurry. This wasn't necessarily intentional and at first, they would run to hide when he first stepped into the room, or closed a cupboard, but sure enough, they eventually just moved a little when he walked into the room, and now I can just open the door to the room, walk straight through and Onyx and Luna are lying in the open, legs kicked backed without even flinching, they are completely relaxed. This is what we're aiming for, and it is so nice to see they don't live in fear anymore.

The golden rule of taming: Remember that guinea pigs are drama queens

If there's anything you take away from this chapter on taming, let it be that guinea pigs are drama queens. They will always make something seem worse than it really is, and this can often put us into panic mode. It is natural for us to be careful around them, after all they are delicate, small creatures. As children we were taught to touch small animals very softly and carefully and not to make loud noises around them. This is right, but we can take this too far, to the point where we stop picking them up and taking them out of their enclosure, can't bond with them and in some cases leave their nails to grow too long because we're too worried we're going to hurt them.

Guinea pigs can be delicate, you need to hold them correctly and safely and no they don't like their bums being touched and never will. However, they can enjoy time outside of their enclosure and sitting on laps for a stroke. They will feel much better with their nails trimmed and will forget about it as soon as it's done.

Do you remember ever crying as a child because you tripped over? It really wasn't that serious, but you've seen blood on your knee and suddenly it's the end of the world! We grow out of this, of course, and the more falls we have the more resilient we become. It's a little bit like this with guinea pigs. They will make such a fuss the first time you pick them up or trim their nails, but eventually will realise it's not so bad because, guess what, nothing bad happened and they're still alive.

The sooner you realise this the better.

You'll have already found out from this book how to keep your guinea pigs happy and how to read their body language. They should never be put in an uncomfortable situation that isn't necessary. But we're talking about things they will really enjoy in life like being stroked and coming out of their enclosure to explore. There are also things that they won't enjoy but are important in keeping them alive and healthy such as handling them enough to pick up on illnesses and taking them to the vets when needed. You don't want the first time your guinea pig is picked up and handled to be at the vets; that's one way to assure they learn that being handled isn't fun after a scary car drive, hearing and smelling dogs in the waiting room and finally a poke and prod from a stranger. They will be fine, though, I promise!

* * *

Below, I'm going to tell you my top 5 taming tips. Put these into practice, and you will find that your guinea pigs have far less to fear, and rather than running away from you, they will be running towards you for food and attention!

1. Allow them to hide, but still see you.

The first common mistake I see all the time is hideaways that are completely closed off. So, when the owner enters the room, the guinea pigs run and hide to a place the owner can't see them. If you can't see them… they can't see you… to them, you *could* be a predator, and they will keep believing that as long as they can't see that you're coming to bring them vegetables. A temporary, or permanent, solution to this is to cut multiple large holes in cardboard boxes, so that they can still hide underneath, but can still see you. This will also make picking up in tip 5 easier and less of a wild goose chase. As they become confident, reintroduce any hideaways you like; they will be happy to come out and see you as they recognise the sounds.

2. Find their favourite food and use it as bait.

They might not be taking food from you straight away, but this can sometimes be because you might not be offering the most delicious and tempting treat. Find their favourite food by giving them a range of fresh fruit and veg to try. Simply place a cup of a variety down and see which they go for first. Every guinea pig is different, but the way to their hearts is through food. Hand feeding them is a great way for them to associate you with food and can be used in trickier situations like health checks, nail trims, or calming them on a trip to the vets.

3. Stroke them gently on the head, but only for a moment.

The trick with stroking your guinea pig isn't to chase them around trying to touch them and frightening them; you need to be slow and gentle and take your hand away from them before they run. This is the key to them realising that stroking them doesn't mean they're going to be picked up or eaten. The best place to do this is on their nose/top of their head. Most guinea pigs will actually like this, and some even like a rub under their chin like a cat does, and some will enjoy their ears being stroked. They don't like their backs near their bums being touched and you will hear some funny noises and might even get a little kick back if you try this and that's one way to make sure they run away from you. You will probably find that when you first reach down to stroke their nose they run away, probably to a corner. Slowly follow them with your hand (slowly is important here), allow them to run away again, and keep trying and eventually you will be able to stroke their nose. Do it for a short moment and move your hand away. Repeat this multiple times a day and your guinea pig will start to realise that it isn't as bad as they thought.

4. Bond with them outside their enclosure.

Exposing them to different environments can be a great way to boost their confidence. A simple playpen set-up or sat on your lap in a different room of the house will introduce them to new sights, sounds and smells that they will soon realise aren't going to harm them. To transport them you don't need to pick them up with your hands. Simply place a pet carrier (front entrance, not top opening) or tunnel inside that they can walk into themselves, close it, pick it up and make sure they can't escape while you're transporting them. Then you can place the pet carrier or tunnel inside the playpen and let them come out in their own time. The first few times you do this you might find that they're too scared to come out. Sometimes they will need some gentle encouragement such as fresh veg, or to place them under a hideaway as mentioned in tip 1 that is quite open. Once they see what's around them (veg and more hideaways) they'll start to explore.

You will always get one guinea pig that will naturally be more confident to do this. Onyx has never been shy to explore, whereas Luna would always stay in one place. It's taken Luna years to get to the point where she will come out and explore, and once I remove her from the pet carrier, she is quite happy to relax and eat vegetables. Eating and cleaning themselves is a sign that your guinea pigs are relaxed and letting their guard down, since they're not things they would do when they think a predator is around.

Sitting with them on your lap could become part of their daily veggie time. That way they can begin to associate this time with you in a positive way. I'd recommend you have more than 1 guinea pig out together, it will help them feel more relaxed.

NB: Children can enjoy guinea pigs on their lap if supervised at all times, but never let a child under the age of 10 pick up or transport a guinea pig since a fall can seriously damage their spine and even be fatal. You might not even want to allow older children to do this and of course use your own judgement on this. Sit the child down first, before putting the guinea pig onto their lap.

5. Practise picking up your guinea pigs.

Onyx absolutely hates being picked up, most guinea pigs do, but she is by far one of the most confident guinea pigs I've met, yet she is the worst at being picked up and will screech as if someone is about to kill her. Once she's on my lap, she immediately flops with her legs kicked out loving the fuss and attention. Guinea pigs will never enjoy being picked up as it's too much like being scooped by a predator, however, you can make the process less stressful and easier for yourself and your guinea pigs. You can of course transport them in a tunnel or pet carrier, there is no real reason to pick them up with your hands. If you do decide to pick them up with your hands for whatever reason, my best tip for this is pick them up facing you and put them down facing you. This is because now they can't see an escape route to jump out of your hands. This will stop a lot of the scrabbling away that they do once you put them down. Always support their front paws and bum and never grab them around the middle with their back feet dangling (that's one way to seem even more like a bird of prey!). Once you've picked them up, hold them close to your body and allow them to sit horizontally since most guinea pigs don't enjoy being held vertically (you might get a nip if you do!), never lie them on their backs. There's a bonus video guide on this in the free gift at the end of the book which I'd recommend watching to make picking up your guinea pigs safe and easy.

My guinea pig still doesn't like being picked up.

That's completely normal! It's very rare they will enjoy being picked up, even in a tunnel or pet carrier.

However, it is necessary for them to be handled for us to check on their health and pick up on illnesses as early as possible, and of course they may enjoy the attention once they're on your lap or roaming around in a play pen. It's a bit like getting an injection, nobody really wants one, but it does us good and causes less stress in the future. So make it as comfortable for them as possible and find which method works best.

Picking up your guinea pigs takes a lot of practice, and it is normal to find one easier to pick up than another. When I first got my guinea pigs I was chasing after them like a headless chicken and would give up, but with practice it can take as little as a second or two.

Don't feel disheartened if it isn't easy, you will eventually find a knack to it; I have a particular corner I like to scoot them into and make sure their things are out of the way. Using two cupped hands I move towards them; they don't have anywhere else to go and I quickly scoop them up. If they're particularly tricky, I learned from my years volunteering at a fox rehabilitation centre, that placing a towel gently, but quickly, over a fearful animal's face can really calm them down and stop them panicking or becoming aggressive; this works well with rodents too, particularly if you're worried about being bitten, so give that a go.

Chapter summary

Taming can take anywhere from hours or weeks to months or years. They will naturally become tamer with time, but there are definitely things you can do to prevent them living in fear and make it easier to trim their nails and check on their health when needed.

Guinea pigs are amazing at learning by association. They're not the brightest of rodents, but give them a routine and the confidence and they will be 'wheeking' for your attention every time they hear your footsteps with the 5 tips in this chapter.

Top 5 taming tips recapped:

1. Allow them to hide, but still see you – adjust your cage layout and get rid of closed off hideaways.
2. Find their favourite food and use as bait – this will make you much more appealing!
3. Stroke them gently on the head, but only for a moment – let them realise they don't need to run away. Don't chase after them to persist in stroking them. Leave them and try later.
4. Bond with them outside their enclosure – floor time or sitting on your lap can be a great way to get on their level and feed veggies.
5. Practise picking up your guinea pigs – scoot them into a corner and pick them up (and put them down) facing you so they won't try to scramble away. Again, don't persist, go back later.

Remember: With new guinea pigs, always give them at least 48 hours to settle in without handling them. This can go a long way in the taming process.

Tame guinea pigs can of course get us more cuddles with our piggie children, but it will also come in handy with the next chapter, where I tell you everything you need to know to make sure your little critters are as healthy as possible.

CHAPTER 9
How to Know if Your Guinea Pig Is Healthy

You might be surprised to hear that guinea pigs can get all sorts of illnesses, from chest infections to bladder stones, infected wounds to tumours. Much of this book will help you keep your guinea pig healthy, but no matter what, sometimes they will still become ill. This chapter will help you to identify some of the common signs and symptoms of illnesses that will allow you to recognise when they need to see a vet and stop problems becoming worse and more expensive down the line.

As prey animals, one of their best ways to defend themselves is to hide illness. Predators will always go for the weakest link; therefore, the better the guinea pig can hide this, the more chance they have of survival.

In a domestic situation, this means it can be difficult for us humans to tell whether a guinea pig is sick.

In this chapter I'll be telling you everything you need to know to check your guinea pig is healthy, and when you need to see a vet.

I am not a vet, and you're probably not either. So don't worry, this isn't going to be a science lesson on how to treat your guinea pigs, but how to spot problems and act on them so that you can rest assured knowing you're taking the best care of your piggies.

When you first get your guinea pig(s) – book them for a general health check with your chosen vet. This starting point will help you know what a healthy guinea pig looks and acts like. And importantly, pick up on any initial health issues.

Do guinea pigs need vaccinations?

Unlike dogs, cat and rabbits, guinea pigs do not need any vaccinations as they aren't susceptible to diseases like myxomatosis. This doesn't mean they can't get sick, of course, and there are certainly things you can do weekly, or even daily to make sure they are healthy.

Should I get my guinea pig neutered or spayed?

Neither are necessary, but here are some reasons you might want to consider neutering your boar or spaying your sow.

A neutered boar can be easily matched with a sow, and it means this can be a successful pairing minus the baby guinea pigs. Neutering is more of a straightforward process than spaying, and therefore people often tend to neuter their boy rather than spay the girl.

Spaying has typically been seen as a risky procedure, so it isn't common. However, some experienced exotic vets are now recommending this as it means she won't get ovarian cysts or uterine tumours in the future, which can tend to happen after the age of 3.

In some parts of the world, even neutering a male isn't a commonly practised procedure and is not at all recommended. So if you're reading this from afar, please note that in the UK neutering is a common procedure. That doesn't mean it doesn't come with its risks, so make sure you find a good exotic vet with plenty of experience with this procedure and discuss the pros and cons.

I cannot stress enough the importance of an experienced exotic vet in this situation.

Can I just visit any vet?

Many vets in the UK will happily see and even operate on a guinea pig, but they won't necessarily all have had the same extensive training specifically in guinea pigs.

Most vets are trained in cats and dogs, with a very small portion on rodents or other pets. For this reason, rodents, along with rabbits, reptiles and more are considered as 'exotic pets' in the veterinary world.

That isn't to say you won't find a regular vet who happens to own guinea pigs and be extremely knowledgeable on guinea pigs, but an exotic vet will have had extensive training and be the best option.

Therefore, it is important to know your vet's reputation and background, especially with more serious issues.

You may not have an exotic vet locally to you, but it is certainly worth finding out, and at the least find out which vet closest to you has the most experience with guinea pigs.

You may be very lucky not to need the vet throughout one of your guinea pig's lives, but it is almost guaranteed at some point, and at times, it is when you least expect it, so I recommend keeping some numbers at hand just in case.

Phone numbers you should keep handy:

- Your local vet (exotic if possible)
- Your local emergency (out of hours) vet

How do I know if my guinea pig is sick?

"What is this on my guinea pig's nose?"

"Do my guinea pigs have mites?"

These are just some of the common questions I see daily in guinea pig forums. When I type in 'Is my guinea pig…' on Google, it comes up with 'pregnant', 'dying', 'overweight', 'in shock', the list goes on.

It is normal to wonder these things, and sometimes we might even think it is silly to ask, and by not asking we may run the risk of ignoring something that *is* a problem.

You and I are not vets, and our jobs are not to treat our guinea pigs ourselves. As owners, it is our responsibility to make sure animals in our care get veterinary attention, when necessary, which of course we are going to. But the real question is, how do we know when something requires a vet and when it doesn't?

I remember the moment I panicked when I saw Luna had a patch of hair missing behind her ears. I frantically googled it to check she didn't have a deadly disease and was relieved to find out this was completely normal. I would have been happy to have taken her to the vets to be told she was fine, and I've had that on many occasions with my pets, but it would have been nice to know and at the very least saved me the worry!

In this chapter you will learn what is a cause for concern and how to check your guinea pig's health, which will allow you to act upon symptoms early and give your guinea pigs the best chance of recovery.

What does a healthy guinea pig look like?

A healthy guinea pig doesn't just have a healthy physical appearance, but also has healthy and normal behaviour.

Healthy physical appearance:

- Shiny, clear, open eyes, occasional white liquid secretion
- Clear breath through a clear nose
- The occasional sneeze or cough is OK
- Solid oval-shaped poos
- Cloudy white urine
- Clean ears, a small amount of dead skin is fine, a furless patch behind the ear is normal
- Smooth, shiny fur
- White, straight teeth of the same length (2 at the top and 2 at the bottom are visible)
- Clean genitals
- Grease/scent gland can feel greasy (positioned low on their back towards their bums)
- Easy movement in the legs
- Smooth feet, slightly pink (or black if they have black feet)
- Nails have a very slight curve
- Consistent weight, a small fluctuation of 30g each week is normal
- Healthy behaviour:
- Healthy appetite
- Normal noises
- Normal personality

What does an unhealthy guinea pig look like?

Below is a list of unhealthy signs, in which you might notice only one or a combination of these when your guinea pig is ill. You may even notice something that isn't on the list, and the key thing is whether it is 'normal' for your guinea pig or not. If you notice any of the below signs, then call your vet for medical advice.

Unhealthy physical appearance:

- Breathing through the mouth
- Lots of sneezing or coughing
- Very dry, small poo, or very wet and soft poo or diarrhoea
- Gritty texture to urine
- Wet, crusty, swollen or closed eye
- Dirty, crusty ears
- Flaky, crusty skin
- Matted fur
- Overgrown or chipped teeth
- Wet or crusty nose
- Abnormal discharge from genitals
- Scabbed or sore grease gland
- Lumps in the body
- Stiff joints
- Inflamed, sore feet
- Overgrown, curved nails
- Sudden weight loss of 80g or more in a week

Unhealthy behaviour:

- Unusual noises such as repetitive sneezing or coughing
- Hunched posture
- Lack of the usual noises you hear

- Lack of appetite
- Change in personality

How do I check my guinea pig's health, and how often?

The best way to check on your guinea pig's health is to observe them each day; when you're feeding them and cleaning them out, just being around them, you will gradually get to know what is normal for them.

Let's say you have a confident guinea pig who will always run up to pull veg from your hand each morning, and another that is shy and takes their time to come out and cautiously find their food when you step away. If that confident guinea pig one morning came out shyly like the other, that would be cause for concern. This was the first sign I had from Wiggy when he was unwell, and sadly passed a week later.

It's really all about knowing what's normal for them and noticing any *changes*.

Changes in weight can also be a good indicator that something might be wrong too. A healthy adult guinea pig can weigh anything from 700-1200 grams, males typically weighing more than females. Much like humans, there can be a perfectly healthy range of weights. However, guinea pigs suddenly losing 80g or more in weight could indicate they're not eating, which could mean they're not well. To check their weight, simply place a towel in a bowl on kitchen scales and place your piggie in the bowl. They might fidget a bit, but should settle enough to get a reading. Record this weight (weekly if you can remember) and if you're ever in doubt about their health this can help you decide if a check-up at the vets is needed.

If you aren't sure, but think something isn't right with your guinea pig, there is no harm in seeing a vet. The peace of mind is worth the cost of a trip to the vets. I would certainly rather have wasted money on a consultation than to have an illness develop and wish I had taken them sooner.

You will be able to check closer the more you sit with your guinea pigs in your lap, which is why it's not just great for bonding but beneficial to their health. You can check for lumps as you stroke them, have a quick peek in their ears and part their fur to see their skin.

There are of course things you can only check from physically handling your guinea pig, such as checking their teeth and genitals. If you're unsure how to handle them safely and comfortably then visit www.littlecrittercare.co.uk/freegift for a video guide where I explain how I do a full health check on my own guinea pigs.

Grooming

Since guinea pigs don't need to take regular baths like humans, self-grooming is something they need to maintain to keep them healthy. However, being domesticated pets, there are a few things that we need to do for them to keep them healthy too.

Unlike their wild relatives, they don't have the same habitat that keeps their nails ground down, and some guinea pigs have been bred as show guinea pigs to have long fur that can be impractical and require human intervention.

So, does my guinea pig need grooming?

Yes, guinea pigs all need some sort of grooming.

When nails grow too long, it alters the way they walk, which in turn causes joint problems and pain walking. The quick (blood supply to the nail) grows as the nail grows, and so if left too long, the nails are more likely to bleed when cut. This chapter will give you some top tips I've learnt from running my home grooming service.

Long-haired varieties of guinea pigs can require daily brushing just like long-haired cats and dogs. Not keeping up with this routine can lead to painful matting which then needs to be cut away, exposing their delicate skin. There'll be more on this, too, so keep reading.

The Teddy breed of guinea pigs, along with some others, tend to have a build-up of dry skin in their ears, which can be loosened and removed with a little olive oil on a cotton bud being careful not to clean inside the ear itself, but only the flaps of skin. Pushing the cotton bud inside the ear could do more harm than good.

Overall, most breeds just need a regular nail trim (every 4–6 weeks) and a light brush. They may even wear down their nails slightly if they're on concrete, which may make a trim less frequent.

Nail trimming

It can sometimes be a daunting thought to put nail clippers close to your guinea pig, and one of the biggest fears is cutting too short and hurting them.

One of my Little Critter Care duties is to visit and trim the nails of local rabbits and guinea pigs. I've trimmed hundreds of nails over the years (I even racked up 6k views on YouTube trimming my tiny hamster's nails). I can honestly say I've cut the quick only 3 times, and the guinea pigs were less bothered about it than me.

Here are my top tips for keeping piggie toes trim:

1. Use a standard pair of toenail clippers
2. Get them sitting comfortable on your lap
3. Have some of their favourite veg on hand to distract them
4. Have some styptic powder, flour, or corn starch on hand to stop bleeding (just in case)
5. Cut about 1–2mms away from the quick
6. Black nails: don't bother trying to see the quick with a torch, just trim the tiniest bit off at a time and aim for the natural curve of the nail. Little but often is best
7. When they pull their foot away, just try again, or try with a different foot. You can always come back to it later
8. Give them a little head rub or veggies in between to calm them down

Tip 4 is an important one, but not because you really need to use it. Simply having it there should help your confidence. Remember, even the best of us cut the quick occasionally and it really isn't a big deal. Just pop some on to stop the bleeding and you and your piggie will be fine.

Should I bathe my guinea pigs?

A bath usually isn't necessary, but being such poop machines, you can sometimes find they've got some poo stuck in their fur, or maybe a hormonal piggie has got quite a greasy scent gland which is clogging up the fur. You might even be recommended to bathe them by your vet if you are treating a fungal infection, or they need some help cleaning themselves.

Baths aren't something guinea pigs particularly enjoy, and so if it's not necessary, don't bathe them.

However, if you think your guinea pig is dirty and needs a bath, here are some tips:

1. Give long-haired breeds a trim to keep their hair from dragging along the floor and free from urine – this might save the need for baths altogether
2. Use a cruelty free, guinea pig safe shampoo such as 'Gorgeous Guineas' from www.gorgeousguineas.com
3. Put a towel down in the bowl or sink so that they have something to grip on to and feel safer
4. Be careful not to get water in their eyes and in their ears

Grooming long-haired guinea pigs

If you have a long-haired guinea pig, you will need to brush their hair regularly (daily to weekly depending on the hair) to make sure it doesn't form into painful matts).

Guinea pigs can squeal when having their hair brushed as it isn't always pleasant for them. To combat this, rather than using a standard small pet comb, try a children's detangler brush. This worked wonders for Wiggy and his long hair.

If brushing is proving to be uncomfortable for you and your guinea pig, doing a hair trim once a month or so can reduce the amount of time you spend brushing.

To trim hair, you can either use a pair of scissors designed for cutting human hair, pet-safe scissors, or even an electric razor. Never let children do this, and if you're unsure please see a local groomer (dog groomers will often help with nail and hair trims for guinea pigs), a local guinea pig rescue, or me for hands-on help if I'm local to you.

You will want to keep some fur so that their skin is protected, and their body temperature is regular, however, you can do just a trim so that the hair is off the ground, or go in with a guarded razor and trim the lot. Avoid the face and ears and be careful of the legs.

In order to keep your guinea pig safe, always pinch the hair between your fingers, and cut on the side away from your guinea pig so that the scissors never encounter their skin. Your guinea pig might make a sudden movement so be careful.

Electric razors are great for this because they're harder to cut yourself or your guinea pig with, and you can still apply the same method of placing the hair between your fingers and then going along your fingers with the electric razor. The guinea pig may of course not like the noise of the electric razor, and so sometimes switching to scissors is best.

Boar cleaning

Boars have an anal sac, which is a little pocket that can get filled with a poo and is completely normal. If this fills with a lot of poo and is hard and smelly in this area, then this might be an 'impaction' in which it may keep filling up and need emptying.

I wouldn't advise poking around this area on your own accord, so if you think something is wrong, please see your vet as you could make things worse by prodding around.

It isn't necessary to clean a boar's anal sac or penis, and many people keeping boars over the years have never needed to do this. It might be more common amongst rescues who are taking in neglected guinea pigs, however, with a clean environment this isn't a problem you should come across, and if you do, an exotic vet should be able to provide you with a simple and safe solution.

If you're finding it difficult to groom your guinea pigs yourself and you'd like a clearer guide, then visit www.littlecrittercare.co.uk/freegift for a stress-free video guide on everything you need to know to groom them safely. Or if you're local to me, you might even like to book your piggies in to a special at-home Guinea Spa session of mine!

Vet bills

My Christmas Day at the emergency vets

We all know 2020 was a total flop, but I am going to tell you how 2020 landed me an extra dollop of poo just to top it off.

A couple of days before Christmas, I noticed Wiggy wasn't acting himself. He wasn't running up to me when I entered the room. Thankfully with all the taming I'd done this was easy to spot quickly.

So, off to the vets we went! He was still eating and drinking at this time, and the vet suggested trying a few basic medications to start and see how he gets on. He seemed to have perked up a little, but by Christmas Day it was clear he had started to go downhill when he was becoming more lethargic and even had started to have diarrhoea.

I knew I had to act immediately, and of course being Christmas Day, many vets were shut, but thankfully there were emergency vets open.

For a consultation and a few medications, it was a little under £200, and with the previous visit, I had spent about £300 at this stage.

At home, with lots of syringe feeding and medications, Wiggy had sadly lost all appetite. We waited with fingers crossed for him to make it until the exotic vet opened almost a week after his strange behaviour started.

I would love to say it was the third vet lucky, but sadly, after making it to the exotic vet, X-ray, blood test and 2 overnight stays with fluids, he didn't make it.

The overall amount I paid that week was about £700. Had he needed an operation, it would have been easily £1000 or more.

I've read many stories where people have spent far more than this. If Wiggy was still around with his suspected heart disease, he would have had to continue ongoing medication which I would have gladly paid for in the hope of extending his life a for couple more years.

Should I get my guinea pigs insured?

Do you insure your car? I assume so, even if it might be only because you legally have to. I've owned some completely worthless cars in the past, however, if I hit a Ferrari by accident, there is absolutely no way I can afford to even fix a small scratch! Have I ever had to use my car insurance? Never, but it gives me peace of mind in case something went wrong, and I even like to include some added extras, making sure if my car wasn't roadworthy, I could get a hire car to allow me to get to the various rabbits, guinea pigs and cats that are waiting to be fed whilst their owners are away.

You can absolutely get insurance for guinea pigs. Pet plans are unusual since guinea pigs don't require vaccinations like rabbits do. However, it is worthwhile at least looking into insurance for guinea pigs. You may need to look for exotic pet insurance, and weigh up the pros and cons.

The question you need to ask yourself is, if you had a sudden emergency and you were quoted £1000, or even £100 or more to potentially save your guinea pig, would you: 1. be able to pay it? or 2. be willing to pay it?

I know that insurance companies make money, and that overall, they will bring in more money than they pay out. I was always under the assumption that as long as I have money saved for my pets, should they need any help, I could pay it and therefore did not need insurance.

But the deciding factor for me was really when I was quoted £1000 for an X-ray and hospitalisation for Wiggy by the emergency vet. Could I have paid it? Yes. Did I want to pay that much knowing his chances were so slim? I had to seriously think about this, and decided unless they were an exotic vet, it was extreme. Had I had him insured, would I have even questioned it? Probably not.

If anything can come from my guilt over this decision, I hope it helps you consider insuring your guinea pigs simply so that you never have to think about the cost of vet bills when it comes to making a decision about your guinea pig's health and well-being. Though do be aware that you will likely have to pay the cost before you claim it back.

The price for me to insure my guinea pigs is about the same as it costs me to insure my economical, small car. And that, of course, can certainly be a monthly cost that isn't possible for everyone, though it might be worth giving up that shop bought coffee each day.

Vets are often very helpful and understand that not everyone can afford treatment, and most will provide a variety of options that can still help your pet and fit different budgets, though they may not always be the option that gives your pet the best chance.

If you are or find yourself in a difficult financial position where you are struggling with vet bills, don't hesitate to seek help. The PDSA (People's Dispensary for Sick Animals) is a charity that can help provide professional veterinary treatment for those that cannot afford it. Many vets also allow you to pay a little later, and you can get credit cards specifically for vet bills. You can even set up a Go Fund Me page where friends, family, and even strangers can help you with the cost.

Pregnancy

"I think my guinea pig is pregnant! Henry is now Henrietta!"

Mis-sexing can be common in pet shops. I remember before I got my first hamster, I had done so much research and decided that a male Syrian would be a good option for me, so off I went to collect Trev from the local pet shop adoption section, only to find out after a few weeks that Trev was a girl (though I decided to keep the name regardless).

This brief section is designed to help those of you who find yourself in this situation. Or maybe it will even prevent the situation happening in the first place if you read this in time.

Intentionally breeding guinea pigs is not advised in any form in this book, however, I recognise that many guinea pig owners can end up in a situation where they have a pregnant guinea pig by accident, or have gone to feed your guinea pigs one morning only to find they have unexpectedly multiplied.

Before you read the rest, I want to explain why I don't advise breeding, just in case you're reading this and think it would be a nice idea (and I know if you're reading this book, you're already the sort of person who will make sure your guinea pigs have the best life).

1. There are thousands of guinea pigs in the UK looking for homes, and rescues are always looking for help. So if you have space for guinea pigs, please help out those in need of homes and I promise you won't regret it.

2. A lot goes into understanding the genetic line of guinea pigs in order to make sure you're breeding healthy guinea pigs. To breed the average guinea pig without knowing their background could mean poor genes being passed down, resulting in sick guinea pigs later down the line.

3. Pregnancy can be life threatening for a guinea pig, and there is a very short window of time that most breeders will breed from sows, and even then, the risk is unnecessary given point number 1.

4. What will happen to the guinea pigs that are bred? Will you keep them? Will they be sold? You cannot plan how many or what genders these guinea pigs will be, and therefore you must be prepared

117

for the maximum litter (up to 8, though common-ly 2–4), and that they may not get on. What will you do if one of the boars fights with the others? Will you really be able to find a good home or will you be putting more strain on rescues?

If you do end up in a situation where you think your guinea pig might be pregnant, or has given birth, then contact your vet and/or a reputable rescue for guidance. They will have the guinea pigs' best interests at heart and will likely have dealt with this situation many times before, and might be able to help you with the extra guinea pigs.

However, if you want some fast information to immediate-ly make sure they are safe, healthy and prevent another pregnancy, here are a few important tips:

- Double check their sex (see page 18)
- Bring the pregnant mother and babies indoors if they are currently outdoors
- Boars (males) should be separated from their mum at 3 weeks or when they weigh 250g, whichever is sooner, as after this they can then reproduce
- Seek expert help in the form of a vet, or reputable rescue

Chapter summary

Whilst I hope your piggies never need to see a vet, more often than not you will at some point come across an ailment with your guinea pigs and need to get them checked out by a guinea pig savvy vet. But after reading this chapter, I hope you're feeling more equipped to deal with an unexpected illness; hey, it might even have saved you that trip to the vets you didn't need because you now know it's normal to have a bald patch behind their ears!

Now you can spend that £30 on some more of their favourite veggies, of course.

If you haven't already, find out where your nearest exotic vet is. If you've not got an exotic vet nearby, or even if you have, it's always handy to find out which vets will happily treat guinea pigs and have a good reputation in your area. Remember that out of hours telephone number too, just in case.

Avoid unnecessary vet visits with my daily, weekly and monthly health check routine:

- Daily – Check on your guinea pigs overall health daily by observation
- Weekly – Do a more thorough check of teeth, genitals and weight weekly
- Monthly – Guinea pigs should have their nails trimmed every 4-6 weeks

It's important to remember that a guinea pigs' mental health is just as important as their physical health. One of the things that will keep them healthy is having their own company, and you might find yourself having to find a new friend for them at some point during guinea pig ownership. So, without further ado, let's find out how to introduce a new guinea pig in the next chapter.

CHAPTER 10
Introducing New Guinea Pigs

At some point you are likely to find yourself looking for another guinea pig to bond with your current guinea pig/s. Maybe you have a single guinea pig, or you already have a group and have the guinea pig bug and you can just never have enough.

For me, despite having both Onyx and Luna still at a prime age, I worried about what would happen if one of them were to suddenly pass away and leave the other alone. As I already had the recommended space for 3, I carefully considered all of the things such as extra vet bills, food and bedding and everything else to think about when getting guinea pigs, and decided to adopt another one! But what gender? What age? What if they don't get along? What if I end up having to separate them and don't have the space? I had lots of questions and worries back then and since 2 successful introductions with guidance from rescues, I am going to share how you can go about this, and I promise it isn't anywhere near as scary as it might seem at first.

Choosing the right pairings

You can't just put any guinea pig with another and expect them to get along. They can be fussy little things, and finding the right friend isn't always straightforward. See Chapter 2 for a table on DO and DON'T pairings.

It is also worth considering the guinea pig's age and health, especially when neutering or spaying comes into it.

Here are some examples you might find yourself in and how you might go about finding a suitable match:

"I have a 2-year-old healthy boar who has fallen out with his companion."

He is young and healthy enough to be neutered by an experienced vet. You could try him with another boar and see how that goes first to avoid neutering, otherwise neutering would almost definitely lead to an easy match with a sow.

"I have a 5-year-old boar who has just lost his companion. He isn't neutered but is healthy."

Due to his age, you might not want to risk neutering. Take advice from a good vet on this one and weigh up the pros and cons. Consider whether he was dominant in his previous pairing. If he was, then you will have a better chance with a more chilled boar, and avoid a young guinea pig who may challenge him in puberty. If he is docile, there shouldn't be too much of a problem finding him a boar friend.

"I have a 4-month-old sow, and realise she needs a friend."

This will probably be an easy match and will probably get on well with a sow or neutered boar of any age.

"I have 2 neutered boars aged 2 and 5."

Unless they are incredibly docile, it's probably unlikely to work with another neutered or unneutered male. Equally, do not attempt to bond with a female. If you would like to care for more guinea pigs you will need at least 2 more in a separate cage. You might even consider getting them a girl each, so that one of the neutered boys lives with a girl in the first cage, and the other neutered boy lives with a different girl in a second cage.

"I have 1 girl and 1 boy who live separately."

You could get the boy neutered, wait 8 weeks, then introduce them. If you do not have an experienced vet and want to avoid neutering, you could get the girl another female companion, and the boy a male companion and keep both pairs living separately.

How to introduce guinea pigs to one another

Guinea pig introductions are not to be taken lightly. There is always the potential for it to end up in a fight and permanent separation. It can be worrying, especially when it is the first time doing an introduction to know when something is going wrong and when something is normal.

When I first adopted Wiggy, I had these same concerns, and fortunately the rescue took those worries away by doing the bonding for me. I dropped off Luna and Onyx at the rescue, where they were to stay for a few nights to be introduced to Wiggy and kept a close eye on. Knowing that they were in experienced hands was such a relief, and I also didn't have the worry that I would take Wiggy home with me only to return him if they didn't get on.

Lots of rescues provide a bonding service, sometimes it is free and sometimes it is a paid service. If you are new to bonding, I would highly recommend you get in touch with a rescue and work closely with them to either have them do the whole process for you or at the very least be on hand for advice if you are attempting it at home.

There are a few different methods that rescues, breeders and owners use to introduce and bond their guinea pigs. With all things, there are different opinions on these and people claiming some methods work better than others.

For me, safety is one of the key factors, as well as making sure they have the best chance of getting along. The information I am about to give on bonding comes from experienced rescues, and is the same method I have used successfully myself. You should find a local rescue you trust to guide you the first time, because as much as this guide will be helpful, you might see a situation unfolding that you can't figure out and need to just ask someone about it that moment. But I hope it can help confirm what you've already been told by your rescue, or be a good reference should you find yourself in a situation where you cannot immediately ask for help and are unsure.

Attempting to bond 2 adult males is never advised for the inexperienced owner; it is more likely to result in a serious injury for the guinea pigs and result in a trip to the emergency vet and costly bills for you. Leave this one to the experts.

Neutral space

Creating a neutral space is the key in creating a successful bond. None of the guinea pigs should have been in contact with the cage or any of its contents beforehand. You can of course clean items that they may have used before, but a special hideaway that one guinea pig particularly loves even if it is clean? Avoid it. It's easy enough to cut some holes in a few cardboard boxes as temporary hideaways. The area for 2 guinea pigs should be at least 1m x 1m. This is a good amount of space that they can get away from one another, but not so large that they have an opportunity to create their own territory. This space can be created with a pen you might use for floor time, or a run you use in the summer. This set up might be there for up to 5 days, so consider where it is placed, ideally somewhere you can regularly monitor them.

Leave nothing to fight over

You should make sure your guinea pigs have nothing to fight over by ensuring there is one of the following for each guinea pig: hideaways (with entry *and* exit holes), water bottles, food bowls (though you can skip this by scatter feeding), and hay piles. Don't use hideaways that only have 1 entrance, as this could cause even the most docile of guinea pigs to react out of fear if they feel cornered should another guinea pig try to enter.

Once you have created this safe neutral space with fresh food and water, place the guinea pigs in together.

Be there to observe behaviour

Take a couple of days off work, or dedicate a weekend to this process in order to make sure it goes as smoothly and safely as possible. You will need to keep a close eye on them particularly for the first 30 minutes or so, and quite possibly longer if there is still tension. Being able to hear them after this will allow you to go about your day but still be on hand to check up on them regularly.

Refer to Chapter 6 on guinea pig noises and body language to help you identify what it going on.

They will need to establish dominance, and so you will likely see behaviours such as chasing, rumble strutting and mounting, and hear noises like complaining/whining, squealing, teeth chattering and purring.

It is normal for it to seem like they are not getting on at times, even with a perfect match. Remember, guinea pigs are drama queens and will make a mountain out of a molehill.

Signs they are getting along:

- Eating in the presence of the other guinea pig
- Exploring and minding their own business
- Backing down when challenged
- Lying down relaxed
- Yawning
- Sitting next to one another

Backing down when challenged doesn't always *look* good but is definitely a good sign. For example, a guinea pig might chase another, the other might run away complaining (backing down), they might even get to the point where the guinea pig being chased gets fed up, turns around and raises their head and shows teeth to the chaser. The chaser turns away and therefore backs down. This is typical of what you might see and is all fine.

Signs that it *might* escalate to a serious fight:

- Continuous teeth chattering that doesn't stop
- Both facing one another with raised heads
- Constant mounting from both
- Relentless chasing that won't give up
- Stopping a guinea pig from eating or drinking

Should I step in to calm things down?

Generally speaking, you need to let them get on with establishing their hierarchy, but if one is persistently bothering the other there are a few things you can do just to divert their attention, which in most cases will work:

- Make a noise: this shouldn't be anything aggressive or to scare them, it is not difficult to startle guinea pigs anyway, so a simple clap of the hands or sudden vocalisation like "hey!" should do the trick.
- Drop in some of their favourite veggies; if the negative behaviour isn't serious, they will often choose to eat something. If they're in a new environment it is normal for them to be a little too nervous to eat though.

Should you have no luck with cooling down the situation with the options above, either they will get over it themselves, or it may be a sign that things will escalate to a fight and you should be prepared to watch closely and intervene.

How do I stop a fight?

Break it up; use something like a dustpan or oven mitt to break up the fight should you see persistent negative behaviours, particularly facing one another teeth chattering and/or raised heads. If you use your bare hands, you risk getting a bite deep enough that you might need to visit A&E, so it's generally not recommended.

What do I do if I need to leave them for a bit?

If they've been displaying good signs of getting along and you haven't seen anything that is close to a fight, you'll be fine to go out, leave them for the night, etc.

However, if there is some tension, and they've been on and off almost fighting or even already had a scuffle, the safest thing to do would be to keep them separated for that time.

Just be aware that doing this will set them back in the introduction process, but that is OK. You will likely see more of the signs at the start of the introductions the first time round again, but it is safer.

How do I know if the bonding has or hasn't worked?

Guinea pigs that get along well enough will show some or all of the 'signs they are getting along' (see above), and never or only rarely (once a week or so) show 'signs that it might escalate into a serious fight' (see above). It is completely normal to see dominant behaviours like rumble strutting, occasional mounting and chasing throughout a bonded pair's lives.

After 48 hours, if the guinea pigs have shown signs they are getting along, and any signs of a fight are no longer there, you're good to place them back into a freshly cleaned enclosure. It is normal for a little chasing, rumble strutting and other dominant behaviours to happen again after this, but it will be very unlikely to escalate after this point.

If you're still seeing some signs for potential fights, give it as long as 5 days if you need to in the neutral space until you stop seeing signs that it might escalate to a fight.

If there has been a fight where blood is drawn, you must permanently separate the fighting guinea pigs. Do not attempt to reintroduce them at any point.

My 2 guinea pigs just keep fighting, and it's time to break them up – what now?

This is a common, but upsetting, situation many people find themselves in, particularly when buying young boars from pet shops. Maybe they've been getting on for years and they've just had a rare falling out that has now made it unsafe to keep them together.

Here are a few options to consider:

- Keep them both, but get them each a cage mate from a local rescue. This will of course take up a considerable amount of more space, time and money than you originally intended, but will ensure all guinea pigs are happy.
- Keep both separately, but directly next to one another. Guinea pigs need company, and sometimes that's even in the form of simply being kept beside the other. This option isn't ideal, but is sometimes necessary once multiple bonding with different guinea pigs have been tried. It is important to remember that 2 individual guinea pigs require more space than they would have had when they were together.
- Keep one, surrender the other to a rescue, and adopt a new friend from the same rescue for your solo guinea pig. This can be a hard decision to make, especially when you have grown to love both guinea pigs equally. It does not take a space away from a rescue and they will be more than happy in helping both guinea pigs find a friend. A reputable rescue will carefully vet adoptees and make sure they go to a good home.

Chapter Summary

Introducing a new guinea pig can be an exciting but nerve-racking time. The truth is, you can never really be sure if it's going to work out, and that's why it's always important to have a plan B in place and ideally a rescue working alongside you. You might also need to be strong willed if you don't have the space for another cage should things not go to plan.

Follow the steps in this chapter when bonding female groups, along with solo neutered male with female groups. Even if you're a beginner at this, this should go smoothly (unless you have a real bossy-boots like boar Onyx).

Remember that adult boars can be tricky, and either you're experienced enough not to need to read this in the first place, or it's worth seeking guidance from someone experienced to hold your hand along the way.

Although it has been great to have lots of choice of guinea pigs from local rescues for my guinea pigs, it's sad that so many end up in rescues because of unsuccessful bonds.

My hope is that the more we adopt rather than shop, we'll not only help guinea pigs in need of homes, but stop new guinea pigs entering rescues because they've not found their match.

CHAPTER 11
Going on Holiday and Leaving Your Pets

Let me tell you a story about the time I came home from holiday to a maggoty hutch!

I was about 10 years old, and me, my mum and brother had gone up to the Midlands to see my grandma. We left my dad in charge of looking after my rabbit, Pepper.

He isn't a massive animal lover, but would have been OK taking on the basic rabbit care jobs for the week that my mum usually did.

In theory, it's a few simple things each day, however, when you look at how much research you're doing, right now, into looking after guinea pigs, it's easy to understand that others might not know even the basics. What do they eat? How much do they need? Do they really need hay constantly or is handful enough? How would you move them when cleaning them out? It's completely understandable that basic pet care can be a minefield, even with the best of intentions.

So… when I got back home from my break away, the first thing I did was run down the garden to the shed, open the hutch and much to my horror, the poo was moving! I burst into tears at the shock of it, I didn't really know what was going on and went to get my mum.

Fortunately, despite the maggots, my rabbit was fine (though it could have easily turned into deadly flystrike), and I'm sure my dad probably got a bit of a telling off.

It was all OK in the end, but imagine if Pepper had become ill. If someone isn't sure about how often to clean out a rabbit in summer, then how would they: 1. notice she was ill in the first place, and 2. get her in a carrier to go to the vets.

And this isn't the only time I've come home to find something's not right with the pet care, with my own pets and clients'. I've taken over pet sitting jobs and found a hutch full of filth, wrong foods being fed by a pro sitter, along with other incorrect care.

I don't believe any of this was down to any intentional neglect, but probably from a lack of education, and instructions not being communicated clearly enough, or simple mistakes.

That being said, there are lots of great options for you to make sure your guinea pigs are well cared for while you're away and prevent any disasters, so that you can relax on holiday too.

This chapter is going to equip you with a range of options available so that you can decide what's best for you and your piggies. There isn't one perfect option for what to do with your pets when you're away. It all depends who is available, what your budget is, how far or how long you're travelling for, or even how many pets you have.

How long is it OK to leave guinea pigs alone for?

As a general rule, no longer than 24 hours. However, you might find you can't leave them even for 12 hours should they finish their hay and water. If you already have guinea pigs, you will understand exactly what I mean when I say they consume a lot more than most people think. Even when I have topped up their hay and water in the morning, I have at times come home only 8 hours later after work to find it's almost gone. Remember, you can never give them too much hay or water.

The reason why they need to be seen to at least every 24 hours is not just for food and water, but to check on their health. Guinea pigs, like other small animals, can go down-hill very suddenly when they start to become ill, and so with the first sign of illness it is important to act immediately and not leave anything too long. Should they become ill, ideally you want to monitor them more frequently and so it is always important to consider this when choosing what to do with your guinea pigs when you're away.

With that in mind, here are some options to consider when going away:

Family and friends

This is a popular option amongst many owners, since it's usually free and doesn't necessarily require moving the guinea pigs.

However, you've already read my previous story so you'll know why that can sometimes be a bad idea.

You might have a family member who already looks after your guinea pigs with you, has their own, or is a real animal lover anyway. If you have these great options, it is still so important to be clear about what is required to care for them.

You might even have a family member who doesn't know much about guinea pigs at all, but can take instructions and is more than happy to help.

The most important question to ask yourself is – if your guinea pig became ill suddenly, would they know this and would they be willing and able to take them to the vets?

After pet sitting for over 5 years, I know that whenever I take on a pet for the week, it's not just down to the time I spend with them, it's being there for when things don't go to plan. Your family member might think it's a straightforward feed and water (which of course most of the time it is!), but just in case, make sure you have things covered.

Neighbours

Neighbours can also be useful to call upon for times when you go away. Particularly if it's only for a night or so, or you're not far away.

Unlike family, neighbours might be less willing to drop things for your pet in an emergency. My advice would always be to have a plan B; such as a friend or family member who might be a little further away but could step in if needed.

If your neighbour suddenly gets invited on a trip and they want to go, are they going to turn it down to look after your pets? Perhaps the neighbour becomes ill and can't continue.

As with family and friends, make sure your neighbour has clear instructions on what to do and how to contact you with any questions.

Pet sitters

A local pet sitter will visit, or even stay overnight with your pets in your own home and carry out anything that needs doing.

This will cost money, of course, but can be very useful as they are usually real animal lovers with lots of experience and are committed to your pets as they would any other job. They won't mind cleaning out your guinea pigs and will usually have lots of experience with this. An experienced pet sitter will be insured, reliable and know what to do in an emergency.

However, sometimes you will find that professional pet sitters work mainly with dogs and cats, and may not know the ins and outs of guinea pig care besides any instructions you give. Communicating with your pet sitter and finding the right person is still really important.

I'd always recommend finding someone who is guinea pig savvy. You may even be lucky enough to have a local veterinary nurse who pet sits, or a guinea pig whisperer like me around!

If you're looking for a pet sitter, see if I'm local to you by visiting www.littlecrittercare.co.uk for the range of services I offer, for little to big critters!

Small pet boarding

A few years ago, when I had 3 hamsters and 2 guinea pigs, one of my hamsters, Ralph, was getting older and had been to the vets a few times. I was so worried to leave him I almost considered cancelling my holiday. I was meant to have a pet sitter or friend come over for visits, but because he might need a sudden vet visit (even if it was to be put to sleep), I booked him in at the local small pet boarding so that I knew he would have someone experienced around most of the time. The others stayed at home for their visits still. He sadly passed away while he was there, but I felt so much better that he was well cared for and had that extra attention.

Rescues, pet shops, and even vets sometimes have small pet boarding facilities and it can be great to have an expert around during the day.

This will of course cost money too, and you will have to transport your guinea pigs a day or so before you go away. For a 2-night trip this can mean a bit of an ordeal to transport them, and not pick them up until the day after you arrive home, however, for a longer trip it could save you money instead of getting a pet sitter who visits your home since you're doing the travelling and not them.

One of the downsides to boarding is that the space can sometimes be less than your pets are used to, as well as travelling to unfamiliar surroundings. In Ralph's case, it was more important that he had expert care, and not his usual large enclosure that he was used to because he was already unwell.

When you have multiple pets, it can work out cheaper to have someone staying overnight with your pets than individually booking them into different places.

Consider when you're packing and getting ready for a flight, do you also have the time to organise your pets into carriers and travel to the boarders? As long as you do, this can be a great option to make sure your pets are safe and well cared for while you're away.

Travelling with your guinea pigs

You can of course, in some cases, take your guinea pigs with you!

This is something I do when I'm staying for a few nights with family at Christmas. It can be a bit of an ordeal and it's not only the pets I must take in their carriers, but their enclosures too.

Wherever you're going must accept guinea pigs too. If it's a family or friend, they might be more inclined to allow them than a hotel will. You can find hotels and B&Bs around that allow pets, but it might also be worth considering whether you want your guinea pigs to be around dogs and other animals that might be unsafe for them.

If you are flying, or travelling a long distance by car, then taking them with you might not be the best idea. Airlines don't tend to allow small pets on board and this would be too stressful to warrant it even if it was possible.

There is no set time for what is appropriate for car journeys. Consider carefully their needs. An hour or so in a small carrier with plenty of hay and cucumber for water content is very different to a hot car for 5 hours without stopping. Think about how often you're able to stop and whether their basic needs will be met.

When guinea pigs are nervous, they might not eat, and so breaks where they can stop without the movement of a car to eat is important as they need to keep their guts moving to be healthy.

When arriving at your destination, a simple playpen with waterproof floor, towels and fleece down can make for a compact and handy temporary enclosure. If you have a C&C cage these grids can be easily flattened and transported too.

Taking your guinea pigs with you on holiday could be the ideal solution for you. It certainly can take more effort, but you'll probably enjoy having them with you. Or maybe you'd love a break from cleaning them out for a week or so a year…

For details on how to travel with your guinea pigs safely, read about this topic on page 39.

Chapter summary

Going away can always be slightly more difficult when you have pets; but it doesn't have to be an ordeal, and you can have a relaxing time away knowing your pets are in safe hands.

Remember that guinea pigs should not be left for more than 24 hours. Even making sure they have lots of food and water won't be enough to make sure they're well; their health is key since they can become ill quickly and it's important to make sure they're not lingering in any unnecessary suffering.

You can keep your guinea pigs in your home by asking others to help, whether that be family, friends, neighbours or a pet sitter.

You might have a local boarding facility where your guinea pigs can stay and have their own holiday.

Or you could even take them with you if you're not going too far and have a suitable enclosure for them to set up at the destination.

Whichever option you decide to go for, plan in advance, and have a plan B, just in case.

And whatever you do, don't expect everyone else to know as much about guinea pigs as you do – be sure to explain their routine and leave emergency details such as your own and vet numbers, and a pet carrier, for when you're away.

CHAPTER 12
Piggie Heaven: What to Do When Your Guinea Pig Passes

Whilst writing this book, I've experienced 2 losses: Wiggy and Sullivan. Because they were sudden, unexpected and somewhat drawn out from illness, I hadn't really had much of a chance to decide what I would do should my guinea pigs pass away. Leaving them with the vet was never something I wanted to do, and burying my pets is always something we'd done since I was young. I remember sobbing as a child from my bedroom window overlooking the garden when my rabbit, Pepper, was buried there. It gave me some comfort to know what had happened and that she was really gone, but was still there in the garden to visit.

However, with renting and moving every few years, burying in a garden didn't necessarily feel like the right option anymore. Unfortunately, when you've had an unexpected loss the last thing you really want to be doing is to be googling all the different options, finding out the pricing, and deciding on something, all whilst you are grieving the loss. At one point, I came across this lovely idea of a clay pawprint, only to see that the delivery would take too long to arrive whilst their body couldn't be kept for long.

The reason I think this most unpleasant part of pet ownership is important to consider early on, is that there are plenty of things you can do whilst they're alive to start making memories and physical things you will be able to keep. It might even be that you save up and keep a pot of money aside for something more costly. Guinea pigs can get surprisingly costly and if you've just footed a big vet bill you may not want to add on a cremation fee at the vets. Below are some options for a variety of budgets that I hope will bring some comfort to you when the sad time comes.

8 ways to remember your guinea pig:

- Take lots of photos and video clips to make memories while they're around.
- Pet-safe pawprint kits (inkless print paper or clay) – this can be done whilst they're still alive and thriving, or if after their death you could even use normal ink or nail polish to get a quick pawprint.
- Get a pet portrait commissioned – this could be a professional photoshoot or a painting or drawing from an artist.
- Pet cremation (communal or individual) – you usually pay more for individual cremation and to have the ashes back. You can then get the ashes turned into something to keep.
- Home burial – you could even mark the spot with a hand-painted stone.
- Pet cemetery – if you don't have a garden yourself or worried about when you move away, a pet cemetery might be a better idea if you want to be able to visit for years to come.
- Plant a special plant or tree to remember them (you could even use their ashes in the soil).
- Create a memory box – photos, a favourite toy, or even a lock of hair.

Also, remember, you don't need to follow the same process for every guinea pig. You may have that one guinea pig that was extra special (the favourite we always say we're not allowed to have, but still do) who we'd like to pay the extra money for to get cremated or even have their ashes made into something, and it's also fine to have those pets we don't feel such a connection with and are OK to leave with the vets after they have passed.

Should you allow your other guinea pigs to see their friend who has passed away?

If your guinea pig passes away in the cage with their cage mates, they likely will have had time to figure out what's going on. But what if your guinea pig has passed away at the vets and you return with their body… will the others like to say goodbye and is it safe?

The important thing is to ask your vet if this is safe to do, since you wouldn't want to be passing anything on to your other guinea pigs that might make them ill.

After Wiggy had been very ill and was back and forth from the vets, Onyx and Luna hadn't been acting themselves and were probably quite confused. So, after the go ahead from the vet after Wiggy's death, I lay Wiggy inside the cage to see what Onyx and Luna would make of the situation.

They were intrigued and concerned, Luna settled quite quickly back to her usual routine of sleeping and eating, however, Onyx spent a solid 20 minutes or so fussing over Wiggy, sniffing, licking and even pulling at his ear at one point. I'm not quite sure what they were thinking or whether it benefitted them in any way, but after giving them enough of their own time to get back to their usual habits I think that might have been their way of understanding. They didn't show any signs of irritated body language or noises, and so I think it was a worthwhile closure for them.

I'm sure they would have been fine and dealt with the change in their own way had they not seen Wiggy, and it's certainly not a necessary step, but it is an option should you decide to let your guinea pigs see their friend's body, safely.

Does your guinea pig need a new friend?

One of the main struggles for owners when one guinea pig of a pair passes, is that one is left alone.

During the mourning process it can sometimes be difficult to think about getting another guinea pig, as of course they won't be able to replace the one you have just lost. However, it is a good idea to start to think about what to do to support your lone guinea pig. A tough question to ask yourself is do you want to keep getting more guinea pigs? If not, is it fair to keep your current guinea pig alone?

In Switzerland, it is illegal to keep only 1 guinea pig, and to support people who have one left there is even a charity that loans out a rescue guinea pig to accompany a lonely guinea pig until their final days. The loaned guinea pig then returns to the rescue to live out the remainder of its life. I always wonder how many people fall in love with the new rescue and so begins the cycle all over again (as you really can't stop once you start)!

Anyway, it can sometimes take a little time to get the ball rolling so it is worth contacting local rescues to explain your current situation. Sometimes you might have a little wait to find the right match for your current guinea pig.

Whilst your current guinea pig is alone, you could always pop in a cuddly toy and move them into a busier part of the home so that they can have more human interaction.

Don't forget to see Chapter 10 if you do decide to get another guinea pig and need some help with pairing and introductions.

Chapter summary

Losing a guinea pig can be more difficult than you think, and remember that everyone in your family will be affected by their death in different ways and even with different guinea pigs. If you're not as upset by their death as you thought you might be, that's also fine.

If you're reading this book, you will have already put in a huge commitment to making sure you fulfil their needs during their lifetime and that's what really counts.

However, there are certainly a few things I wish I'd prepared for, such as taking more photos and even things like pawprints while Wiggy and Sullivan were alive.

There are different ways to remember them, whether that's simply having a photo of them by your bedside, a spot to visit or even just keeping them in your memories.

There also comes a point when you might decide whether or not to continue keeping guinea pigs and what you need to do to support any guinea pigs that might be left alone. This is when local rescues and guinea pig communities will be a huge support and there are lots of options to choose from. If and when you decide to add more guineas to your family, go back to Chapter 10 on guinea pig introductions, which should help that part go smoothly.

Little Critter Lucy's Final Advice

"If I didn't have guinea pigs, my clothes would have no fur, my house would be clean, and my wallet would be full, but my heart would be empty."

Unknown

Waking up in the morning, I hear the comforting squeaks from Onyx and Luna. The first thing I often do before I creep to the bathroom is say "Hi", top up their hay to see their popcorns of joy (as if they didn't have enough already) and watch them eagerly tuck into their breakfast. Coming home from a long day at work I can be sure they've kept themselves busy eating, exploring and lazing around, before they run up to greet me at the end of their cage after more food and a fuss. Evenings can always be spent curling up with them to watch a film, and summer days watching them enjoy time on the grass. Isn't this just the guinea pig owning dream? Achieving this is very possible, you just need to put in the time and effort at the start.

Guinea pigs can provide so much value to our lives, though it doesn't come without its challenges. They do say nothing good in life comes easy, and guinea pigs are definitely worth the work. My hope for this book is that I've helped you truly understand the benefits and challenges of guinea pig ownership. They're certainly not the easy starter pets we're often sold, but owning guinea pigs also doesn't have to be that hard (and it turns out they're way more awesome than we initially thought).

The most important thing you'll learn from this book is that our joy from guinea pig ownership comes from seeing *them* happy and healthy.

I've given you the key foundations that will help your guinea pigs be as happy and healthy as possible so that you can get all of the benefits of guinea pig ownership and less of the stress. My hope is that by helping you make guinea pig ownership easier and more enjoyable; your guinea pigs will benefit just as much as you.

If you agree that I've helped you along your guinea pig owning journey, please leave me a review on Amazon; this will help me reach more guinea pig owners, and therefore help more guinea pigs thrive.

Some key things to action right now would be to make sure your guinea pigs have enough space and places to hide as well as a good diet including vitamin C and a *lot* of hay. Once you have these foundational needs met, build a routine that makes feeding and cleaning super easy; how you have their space arranged plays an important factor in your cleaning routine, ease of picking up as well as their confidence. Remember the easier you can access the places they pee the most, the less of a chore it will become.

You can't learn everything from this book as there's always more to learn. You'll make mistakes along the way too, and that's OK.

You might also need to know how to handle your guinea pig should they need syringe feeding, or get some hands-on practice with nail trimming. You might even want to find out about the variety of foods you can pick from your garden for your guinea pigs, or find ways to save money on buying the best hay and bedding.

To help you, I have put together some free resources for you to enjoy which will help you beyond this book.

Acknowledgements

A massive thank you to my friends for helping me get this book done over the past year.

To my mentor, Dom Hodgson, who I wouldn't have had the idea to write this book without. Thanks for helping me realise the potential to help little critter owners far and wide.

To my friend and incredible illustrator, Bonnie Abhayaratne, for bringing me and my guinea pigs to life on the front cover.

To my proofreader and fellow guinea pig lover, Abbie Rutherford.

To my fabulous Little Critter Care clients who have been so supportive and encouraging of positive changes over the years.

To my mum and dad for getting me started on my animal-obsessed journey with my first rabbit, Pepper, at the age of 4. Thanks for continuing to looking after my pets when I'm away and allowing them to join for Christmas. And an extra thanks to my mum who also helped with proofreading the first draft of this book.

To my patient fiancé, Brett, who despite initially not particularly wanting guinea pigs, is often seen fussing over them and saving them their favourite vegetable scraps from dinner. Me and the pigs thank you for putting up with finding hay and guinea pig hair woven into your belongings.

And finally to you, the reader, for taking time out of your busy schedule to read this book in order to learn more about caring for your guinea pigs, I say thanks. If you got any value, please leave a review for me. I'm passionate about keeping guinea pigs and their owners together and taking the strain off so many amazing rescues, and the best way for you to help me to help them, is to leave a nice review on Amazon.

Lucy

My Free Gift to You

I hope this was an enjoyable read, and I hope it's inspired you to adopt a pair of guinea pigs, or if you already have guinea pigs, given you plenty of ideas to take away.

I appreciate there's only so much you can get from a book, so to help you, I'm giving you free access to a range of bonus videos, guides and an eBook to help you even further.

These bonuses complement various chapters of this book, and will give you more hands-on guidance where you'll be able to watch me and my guinea pigs putting some of these things into practice.

Inside you will get:

- Bonus 1: The easy, budget-friendly guide to your guinea pig cage set-up; see how to lay out your guinea pig enclosure for ultimate popcorning piggie happiness.
- Bonus 2: How to pick up your guinea pig easily and safely: the video guide to help you become a pro at picking up.
- Bonus 3: *How to Potty Train Your Little Critter in 5 Days, No Mess, Less Stress* eBook – this is an extension of one of the chapters in the book, including images demonstrating ideal potty-training layouts.
- Bonus 4: A complete guide to trimming your guinea pigs' nails at home – includes video demonstration methods not seen in the book.

- Bonus 5: How to tame your guinea pig in 5 days: access to videos, Q&A, discussion to help you turn your timid piggie into a confident critter.

To get free, full and immediate access to all of this, simply go to www.littlecrittercare.co.uk/freegift for your solutions.

If you have trouble accessing any of the resources, please email me at littlecrittercaresevenoaks@gmail.com

.

Printed in Great Britain
by Amazon

71899686R00088